There's Alw

SUGAR FREE **JELL-O**

BRAND

INTRODUCTION

THERE'S ALWAYS ROOM FOR SUGAR FREE JELL-O was carefully created to include recipes that taste great but aren't just for dieters! Even though a single serving of a recipe can be as low as 8 calories and no recipe has more than 190 calories per serving, most of the recipes are perfect for serving regularly to your family.

We've included recipes that are great at any time of the day and many are perfect for entertaining. In fact, when you are looking for special occasion recipes, our chapter "Good Enough For Guests" could have just the recipe you want. For chocolate fans, we've included an entire chapter on this enticing flavor. There is also a section devoted to delicious shakes. Any one of these shakes makes a great nutritious treat or a breakfast accompaniment. Another chapter is devoted to "Lunch in a Cup." These inspired entrees are a delicious alternative to salads that often become calorie laden with high-fat dressings or toppings. Because everything is individually portioned, they are particularly well-suited for packing for lunch. Of course, we have also included snacks and salads for which JELL-O Brand products have long been well respected.

All of the recipes in this book were developed with today's healthy lifestyle in mind. JELL-O Sugar Free Gelatin and JELL-O Sugar Free Pudding are low in fat and cholesterol. Every recipe was created to take advantage of these qualities, but never at the sacrifice of taste.

JELL-O Brand Sugar Free products provide an extremely versatile foundation. They offer the perfect base to hold fruits and vegetables without lots of fat and calories. Fat often provides the "structure" that helps hold ingredients together. JELL-O Brand Gelatins and Puddings can provide structure without a lot of fat in a wide variety of recipes ranging from dips and appetizers to delicious desserts. JELL-O Sugar Free products are made with NUTRASWEET® sweetener, which eliminates extra calories from sugar.

Every recipe is easy—in fact, once you've made them, you'll want to make them again and again. None takes more than 30 minutes to prepare (excluding refrigeration and freezing) and most are even faster.

We think you will agree that all of these recipes have a place in your permanent recipe collection.

SANE TALK ABOUT HEALTHY EATING

The United States Department of Agriculture (USDA) and the United States Department of Health and Human Services recently updated the Dietary Guidelines for Americans—seven basic principles that encourage balance, variety and moderation in food consumption. Highlights of each guideline are presented here. (For further information, tips and recipes, write to the Consumer Response and Information Center at Kraft General Foods, 250 North Street, White Plains, New York 10625 for a copy of a new brochure series, ''SANE TALK about Healthy Eating for the 90's the Dietary Guidelines Way.'')

1. Eat a variety of foods

Variety is not only the spice of life, but it is also the secret to making sure that you get the nutrients you need each day. No one food supplies all the essential nutrients. That is why it is important to eat a variety of foods each day to get all the nutrients you need for good health.

2. Maintain healthy weight

Even though many of us are making progress toward more healthful diets, recent studies indicate that one out of every four adult Americans is overweight. While many of us think of being overweight as a problem for reasons of appearance, obesity can be a serious health hazard. It is linked to high blood pressure, diabetes, heart disease, stroke, some forms of cancer and many other medical problems.

3. Choose a diet low in fat, saturated fat and cholesterol

Our bodies need much less dietary fat than most of us currently consume. Health authorities recommend that we get 30 percent or less of our calories from fat. Once you know your daily calorie requirement, it's simple to calculate your recommended fat intake. Just drop off the last digit and divide by three. For example, if your daily calorie need is 1800 calories, drop the last digit (180) and divide by 3 to get 60 grams of fat per day. No more than a third of that, 20 grams, should come from saturated fat. It is recommended that you not consume more than 300 milligrams of cholesterol each day.

4. Choose a diet with plenty of vegetables, fruits and grain products

Health authorities tell us that most Americans are not consuming enough vegetables, fruits and grains. By eating more of these foods, you are likely to increase the amount of complex carbohydrate and dietary fiber and reduce the total amount of fat in your diet.

5. Use sugars only in moderation

The Dietary Guidelines suggest that sugars be used in moderation by most healthy people and sparingly by people with lower calorie needs. Although sugar has been targeted as the cause of several health problems, research has shown that the only health problem that is directly linked to eating sugar is tooth decay. Proper dental hygiene can help prevent this problem. While sugars have a place in the diet, consuming extra sugar above our daily calorie needs can lead to added pounds.

6. Use salt and sodium only in moderation

We get sodium from many sources, but mostly in the form of salt (sodium chloride) added to foods in processing, in cooking and at the table. While some sodium is essential (only about 500 milligrams a day), most Americans consume much more than they need. The National Academy of Sciences recommends a "safe and adequate" limit of no more than 6 grams of salt, which is equal to about 2400 milligrams of sodium per day for adults. Though it has not been proven that eating large amounts of sodium causes high blood pressure, many health professionals believe that reducing sodium intake is a good idea for the population as a whole especially since we generally eat much more sodium than our bodies need.

7. If you drink alcoholic beverages, do so in moderation

According to the Dietary Guidelines, drinking too much alcohol poses risks to health and well being. If you choose to drink, the Dietary Guidelines recommend doing so in moderation.

And don't forget . . . exercise!

An important part of a healthy lifestyle is exercise. Exercise is very important if you are trying to lose weight or maintain fitness. Moderate exercise burns calories and may also curb the appetite and help relieve stress. Exercise is beneficial because it can:

- help you maintain your ideal weight
- increase your stamina
- improve your muscle tone
- relieve stress
- improve your cardiovascular fitness
- make you feel and look good

EXPLANATION OF NUTRITION INFORMATION PROVIDED

The recipes in this cookbook were designed with good nutrition and taste in mind. Nutrition information is provided for each recipe on a per serving basis using the ingredients listed. The nutrient content was calculated using General Foods USA's nutrient database which contains nutrient information for over 15,000 General Foods products and generic foods. In addition to basic nutrition information, diabetic exchanges* are provided for each recipe. Exchange information can also be of use to weight-conscious persons following similar meal plans.

*Exchange lists are the basis of a meal planning system designed by a committee of the American Diabetes Association and the American Dietetic Association. While designed primarily for people with diabetes and others who must follow special diets, the exchange lists are based on principles of good nutrition that apply to everyone.

Exchange calculations based on Exchange Lists for Meal Planning © 1989, American Diabetes Association, Inc. and the American Dietetic Association.

NOTE TO DIABETICS

The majority of recipes in this cookbook can easily be incorporated into your meal plan. Some recipes should be considered "foods for occasional use" because of their higher sugar and fat content. Some recipes contain wines and liqueurs to add extra flavor. These ingredients are optional, but the nutrition calculations include them. **Consult your doctor or dietitian for guidance on how and when the recipes in this book may be included in your particular meal plan.**

SAVVY WITH JELL-O SUGAR FREE PRODUCTS

This is where our professionals share their secrets with you— foolproof tips to ensure great results every time and simple additions guaranteed to add pizzazz to any recipe.

GELATIN POINTERS

Making JELL-O Brand Sugar Free Gelatin is easy. Just follow the package directions and the results are terrific!

The basic directions as written below are also on the package:

Add 1 cup boiling water to 1 package (4-serving size) gelatin. Stir until dissolved, about 2 minutes. Add 1 cup cold water. Chill until set. JELL-O Brand Sugar Free Gelatin can be used in any recipe that calls for JELL-O Brand Gelatin.

Some tips for success

- To make gelatin that is clear and uniformly set, be sure the gelatin granules are completely dissolved in boiling water or other boiling liquid before adding the cold liquid.

- To double a recipe, just double the amounts of gelatin, liquid and other ingredients used except salt, vinegar and lemon juice. For these, use just 1½ times the amount given in the recipe.

- To store prepared gelatin overnight or longer, cover it to prevent drying. Always store recipes made with gelatin in the refrigerator.

- To easily combine whipped topping, yogurt, sour cream or mayonnaise with gelatin, use a wire whisk or fork.

- For best results, use gelatin desserts within three days of preparation.

- Use the appropriate measuring cups for dry and liquid ingredients. Use glass or plastic measuring cups with pouring spouts for liquids. Use nested metal or plastic measuring cups for dry ingredients.

- Use measuring spoons instead of flatware.

How to speed up chilling time

- Choose the *right container*—metal bowls or molds chill more quickly than glass or plastic bowls so your gelatin will be firm in less time. Also, individual servings in small molds or serving dishes will chill more quickly than large servings.

- **Speed set (ice cube method):** Dissolve gelatin completely in ¾ cup boiling liquid. Combine ½ cup water and enough ice cubes to make 1¼ cups. Add to gelatin, stirring until slightly thickened. Remove any unmelted ice. Pour into dessert dishes or serving bowl. Chill. Mixture will be soft-set and ready to eat in about 30 minutes, firm in 1 to 1½ hours. However, do not use this method if you are going to mold the gelatin.

- **Ice bath method:** Dissolve gelatin according to package directions. Place bowl of gelatin mixture in larger bowl of ice and water; stir occasionally as mixture chills to ensure even thickening. In fact, our General Foods food professionals prefer this method because it saves a lot of time.

- **Blender method:** Completely dissolve 4-serving size package of gelatin and ¾ cup boiling liquid in small bowl; pour into blender container. (**Note:** The volume of the 8-serving size package is too large for most blenders.) Combine ½ cup water and enough ice cubes to make 1¼ cups; add to gelatin. Stir until partially melted. Blend at high speed 30 seconds. Pour into individual dessert dishes or bowl. Chill until set, at least 30 minutes. Mixture is self-layering and sets with a frothy layer on top and a clear layer on bottom.

Gelatin Chilling Time Chart

In all recipes, for best results, the gelatin needs to be chilled to the proper consistency. Use this chart as a guideline to determine the desired consistency and the approximate chilling times for a 4-serving package.

When recipe says:	It means gelatin should . . .	It will take about:		Use it for . . .
		Regular set	Speed set*	
Chill until "syrupy"	be consistency of thick syrup	1 hour	3 minutes	glaze for pies, fruits
Chill until "lightly thickened"	be consistency of unbeaten egg whites	1¼ hours	5 to 6 minutes	adding creamy ingredients such as whipped topping, or when mixture will be beaten
Chill until "thickened"	be thick enough so that spoon drawn through it leaves a definite impression	1½ hours	7 to 8 minutes	adding solid ingredients such as fruits or vegetables
Chill until set but not firm"	stick to the finger when touched and should mound or move to the side when bowl or mold is tilted	2 hours	Individual servings or layers: 15 minutes 2- to 6-cup bowl: 30 minutes	layering gelatin mixtures
Chill until firm"	not stick to finger when touched and not mound or move when mold is tilted	Individual molds: at least 3 hours 2- to 6-cup mold: at least 4 hours 8- to 12-cup mold: at least 5 hours or overnight		unmolding and serving

Speed set (ice cube method) not recommended for molding because pieces of unmelted ice may result in pockets of water.

The Secret to Molding Gelatin

The Mold
- Use metal molds, traditional decorative molds and other metal forms, as well. You can use square or round cake pans, fluted or plain tube pans, loaf pans, metal mixing bowls (the nested sets give you a variety of sizes), or metal fruit or juice cans (to unmold from can, dip in warm water, then puncture bottom of can and unmold).

- To determine the *volume of the mold,* measure first with water. Most recipes give an indication of the size of the mold needed. For clear gelatin, you need a 2-cup mold for a 4-serving size package of gelatin.

- If the mold holds less than the amount called for, pour the extra gelatin mixture into a separate dish and serve at another time. Do not use a mold that is too large, since it would be difficult to unmold. Either increase the recipe or use a smaller mold.

- For easier unmolding, spray mold lightly with non-stick cooking spray before filling mold.

The Preparation
- Use less water in preparing gelatin if it is to be molded. For 4-serving size package, add ¾ cup cold water to dissolved gelatin. (This adjustment has already been made in recipes in this book that are to be molded.) This makes the mold less fragile and makes unmolding much simpler.

- To arrange fruits or vegetables in molds, chill gelatin until thickened, then pour gelatin into mold to about ¼-inch depth. Arrange fruits or vegetables in decorative pattern in gelatin. Chill until set but not firm, then pour remaining thickened gelatin over pattern in mold.

The Unmolding
- First, allow gelatin to chill until firm, several hours or overnight. Also, chill serving plate or individual plates on which mold will be served.

- Make certain that gelatin is completely firm. It should not feel sticky on top and should not mound or move to the side if mold is tilted.

- Moisten tips of fingers with water and gently pull gelatin from edge of mold. Or, use a small metal spatula or pointed knife dipped in warm water to loosen top edge.

- Dip mold in warm, not hot, water, just to the rim, for about 10 seconds. Lift from water, hold upright and shake to loosen gelatin. Or, gently pull gelatin from edge of mold.

(continued)

Unmolding Gelatin

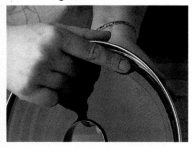

1. Before unmolding, pull gelatin from edge of mold with moist fingers. Or, run small metal spatula or pointed knife dipped in warm water around edge of gelatin.

2. Dip mold in warm water, just to rim, for 10 seconds.

3. Lift from water and gently pull gelatin from edge of mold with moist fingers.

4. Place moistened serving plate on top of mold.

5. Invert mold and plate and shake to loosen gelatin.

6. Gently remove mold and center gelatin on plate.

- Moisten chilled serving plate with cold water; this allows gelatin to be moved after unmolding. Place moistened plate over mold and invert. Shake slightly from side to side, then lift off mold carefully. If gelatin doesn't release easily, dip the mold in warm water again for a few seconds. If necessary, move gelatin to center of serving plate.

Simple additions to make gelatin special

Fruits and vegetables
Chill gelatin until it is thickened, then fold in ¾ to 1½ cups fruits or vegetables. Do not use fresh or frozen pineapple or kiwifruit or fresh ginger root, papaya, figs or guava; an enzyme in these fruits will prevent the gelatin from setting. These fruits are fine, however, if cooked or canned, because these processes break down the enzyme. Canned or fresh fruits should be drained well before adding to gelatin (unless a recipe specifies otherwise). The fruit juice or syrup can be used as part or all of the liquid called for in a recipe.

Carbonated beverages
Substitute cold carbonated beverages, such as club soda, seltzer, fruit flavor sparkling water, or sugar free cola, ginger ale, lemon-lime flavor drinks or root beer, for part or all of the cold water.

Fruit juice
Use fruit juice for part of the cold liquid—orange juice, apple juice, cranberry juice, tomato juice or canned pineapple juice. Use boiling fruit juice if replacing boiling water.

Flavored extracts
Add flavored extracts, such as vanilla, almond, peppermint or rum—just a touch for additional flavor.

Wine or liqueur
Add a little wine or liqueur for a festive touch (too much wine or liqueur will prevent gelatin from setting properly). Use 2 tablespoons white wine, red wine, sherry or 1 tablespoon creme de menthe or chocolate or fruit flavor liqueur.

Ways to add extra flair to gelatin

Whip it
Chill prepared gelatin until thickened but not set. Then beat with a rotary beater or electric mixer at medium speed until mixture is fluffy and thick and about doubled in volume. Chill until firm. To shorten preparation time, chill gelatin using ice bath method (see page 6) until thickened, but not set. Then beat gelatin while still in ice bath.

Flake or cube it

Prepare gelatin as directed on package, reducing cold water to ³⁄₄ cup. Pour into shallow pan and chill until firm, about 3 hours.

- To flake, break gelatin into small flakes with fork or force through a large mesh strainer; pile lightly into dishes, alone or with fruit or a dollop of whipped topping.

- For cubes, cut gelatin into small cubes, using sharp knife that has been dipped in hot water. To remove cubes from pan, quickly dip pan in warm water and invert onto plastic wrap. Serve in dishes with fruit and/or a dollop of whipped topping, if desired.

Layer it

Make layers with different flavors or different types of gelatin mixtures. Chill each layer until set but not firm before adding the next layer; if lower layer is too firm, the layers may slip apart when unmolded. The gelatin should stick to fingers when touched and move gently from side to side when the bowl is tilted. Except for the first layer, the gelatin mixtures should be cool and slightly thickened before being poured into mold; a warm mixture could soften the layer beneath it and cause mixtures to run together.

Tilt it

Fill parfait or any stemmed glasses ½ full with gelatin. Tilt glasses in refrigerator by catching bases of glasses between bars of refrigerator rack and leaning tops of glasses against wall. Chill until set but not firm. Place glasses upright. Fill with additional gelatin as desired. (Use whipped gelatin or another flavor gelatin.) Chill until firm.

PUDDING POINTERS

The recipes in this book use both JELL-O Sugar Free Instant Pudding and Pie Filling, which is not cooked, and JELL-O Sugar Free Pudding and Pie Filling, which requires cooking. <u>These products are not interchangeable in recipes.</u> Be sure to use the product called for in the recipe.

The basic directions as written below are also on the package:

For JELL-O Sugar Free Instant Pudding and Pie Filling:
- Pour 2 cups cold milk into bowl. Add contents of 1 package (4-serving size) pudding mix. Beat with wire whisk or at lowest speed of electric mixer until well blended, 1 to 2 minutes. Pudding will be soft-set, ready to eat in 5 minutes.

- **Shaker method:** Pour cold milk into leakproof 1-quart container. Add contents of 1 package (4-serving size) pudding mix. Cover tightly. Shake vigorously at least 45 seconds. Pudding will be soft-set, ready to eat in 5 minutes.

- **Whisk method:** Place contents of 1 package (4-serving size) pudding mix in 1-quart bowl. While stirring with whisk or fork, gradually add milk. Stir until blended and smooth, about 2 minutes. Pudding will be soft-set, ready to eat in 5 minutes.

- **Blender method:** Pour cold milk into electric blender. Add contents of 1 package (4-serving size) pudding mix; cover. Blend at high speed 15 seconds. Pudding will be soft-set, ready to eat in 5 minutes.

For JELL-O Sugar Free Pudding and Pie Filling:
- Stir contents of 1 package (4-serving size) pudding mix into 2 cups milk in a heavy medium saucepan. Cook and stir over medium heat until mixture comes to full boil. Pudding thickens as it cools. Serve warm or cold.

- **Microwave directions:** Stir contents of 1 package (4-serving size) pudding mix with milk in 1½-quart microwavable bowl. Follow the package directions for your flavor of pudding. **Note:** Ovens vary; cooking time is approximate. Microwave method not recommended for ovens below 500 watts.

For even more recipes, JELL-O Sugar Free Instant Pudding and Pie Filling and JELL-O Sugar Free Pudding and Pie Filling can be substituted for their respective instant and cooked pudding mixes in your other favorite recipes.

Some tips for success

For JELL-O Sugar Free Instant Pudding and Pie Filling:
- Always use cold milk. Beat pudding mix slowly, not vigorously.

For JELL-O Sugar Free Pudding and Pie Filling:
- It's best to cook pudding in a heavy saucepan to ensure even heating. Stir pudding mixture constantly as it cooks. Make sure it comes to full boil. The mixture will be thin, but will thicken as it cools.

- For a creamier pudding, stir before serving.

- To cool pudding quickly, place pan of hot pudding in larger pan of ice water; stir frequently until mixture is cooled.

- For molded pudding recipes, cool cooked pudding 5 minutes, stirring twice; then pour into plain mold or individual custard cups that have been rinsed in cold water. Chill. To unmold, dip mold or cup in hot water.

Always store recipes made with pudding in refrigerator.

INGREDIENT INFORMATION

All of the recipes were carefully tested using the ingredients listed. To duplicate our results (both the final product and the nutrition information), make sure to use the products that are specified.

Milk

Even though skim milk has fewer calories than 2% lowfat milk, we sometimes recommend 2% lowfat milk because it creates a product with a richer, creamier texture, but with fewer calories and fat than a recipe made with whole milk, half-and-half or cream.

Nuts and coconut

Toasting nuts and coconut enhances their rich, satisfying flavors and enables you to use less of these ingredients.

To toast nuts: Spread nuts in a shallow baking pan. Toast at 350°F, stirring frequently, 8 to 10 minutes or until golden brown.

To toast coconut: Spread coconut in a shallow baking pan. Toast at 350°F, stirring frequently, 7 to 12 minutes or until lightly browned. Or toast in microwave oven on HIGH, 5 minutes for 1⅓ cups, stirring several times.

Neufchatel cheese and pasteurized process cream cheese product

Several of our recipes call for neufchatel or pasteurized process cream cheese product.

For the neufchatel cheese, we used KRAFT Neufchatel Cheese OR Light PHILADELPHIA BRAND Neufchatel Cheese. Both of these products come in 8-ounce boxes.

For the pasteurized process cream cheese product, we used Light PHILADELPHIA BRAND Pasteurized Process Cream Cheese Product. It comes in an 8-ounce plastic cup. This should not be confused with "soft" or "whipped" cream cheese which also comes in an 8-ounce cup.

Reduced-calorie sour cream

When we call for reduced-calorie sour cream, our nutrition information is based on SEALTEST LIGHT Cultured Sour Half-and-Half. Other reduced-calorie sour cream products can be substituted, but the nutrition information will vary slightly.

SNACK ATTACKS

Snacks are often a dieter's downfall. With the help of recipes from Sugar Free JELL-O, you'll be well armed the next time the munchies strike. Every recipe in this chapter can easily be made in individual servings so it's simple to have portion-controlled snacks on hand at all times . . . over half the recipes have 50 calories or less per serving.

Having these recipes on hand could help prevent you from eating popular snacks that tend to be high in fat and calories. The rich, creamy taste and texture of Cherries Jubilee at 120 calories per serving can help ward off a hankering for eating a higher calorie dessert. Other recipes in this chapter are particularly good for satisfying a desire for something cool and refreshing even though they have very few calories. For instance, a serving of Melon Bubbles featured on the opposite page contains only 14 calories.

To help you with your dieting efforts, make sure to stock your refrigerator and freezer with these easy-to-make snacks, so the next time you have a snack attack there will be a sweet treat ready to come to your rescue.

Melon Bubbles (page 16)

Melon Bubbles

Substitute orange juice or pineapple juice for the cold water for additional flavor and about 25 extra calories per serving.

1 package (4-serving size) JELL-O Brand Sugar Free Gelatin, any flavor
¾ cup boiling water
½ cup cold water
Ice cubes
1 cup melon balls (cantaloupe, honeydew or watermelon)

- Completely dissolve gelatin in boiling water. Combine cold water and enough ice cubes to measure 1¼ cups. Add to gelatin; stir until slightly thickened. Remove any unmelted ice. Measure 1⅓ cups gelatin; add melon. Pour into 7 individual dishes or medium serving bowl.

- Beat remaining gelatin at high speed with electric mixer until thickened and doubled in volume. Spoon over gelatin mixture in dishes. Chill until set, about 2 hours. Garnish if desired.

   Makes 3½ cups or 7 servings

Nutrition Information Per Serving:			
Calories	14	Fat	0 g
Cholesterol	0 mg	Carbohydrate	2 g
Sodium	50 mg	Protein	1 g

Diabetic Exchanges Per Serving:
Free, Limited

Cherries Jubilee

There's nothing dietlike about this delectable dessert.

1¼ cups cold 2% lowfat milk
½ teaspoon almond extract, divided
1 package (4-serving size) JELL-O Vanilla Flavor Sugar Free Instant Pudding and Pie Filling
2 tablespoons sliced toasted almonds, divided
1 cup thawed COOL WHIP LITE Whipped Topping
1 can (20 ounces) reduced-calorie cherry pie filling

- Pour milk and ¼ teaspoon of the extract into large mixing bowl. Add pudding mix. Beat with wire whisk until well blended, 1 to 2 minutes. Chop 1 tablespoon of the almonds; gently stir into pudding mixture with whipped topping.

- Mix cherry pie filling with the remaining ¼ teaspoon extract. Alternately spoon pudding and cherry pie filling mixtures into parfait glasses. Refrigerate until ready to serve. Sprinkle with the remaining 1 tablespoon sliced almonds.

   Makes 8 servings

Nutrition Information Per Serving:			
Calories	120	Fat	3 g
Cholesterol	5 mg	Carbohydrate	22 g
Sodium	200 mg	Protein	2 g

Diabetic Exchanges Per Serving:
1½ Fruit, ½ Fat

Cherries Jubilee

Muffin Pan Snacks

Keep a tray of these in your refrigerator to have on hand for quick snacks. In place of the orange and carrot, try any of the variations below. (The nutrition information applies to the ingredients listed in the recipe.)

1 package (4-serving size) JELL-O Brand Sugar Free Gelatin, any flavor
¾ cup boiling water
½ cup cold water
 Ice cubes
1 medium orange, peeled and cut into bite-size pieces
¼ cup shredded carrot

- Completely dissolve gelatin in boiling water. Combine cold water and enough ice cubes to measure 1 cup. Add to gelatin; stir until slightly thickened. Remove any unmelted ice. Add orange and carrot. Chill until thickened, about 10 minutes.

- Place foil baking cups in muffin pans, or use small individual molds which have been lightly sprayed with non-stick cooking spray. Spoon gelatin mixture into cups, filling each cup about two-thirds full. Chill until firm, about 2 hours. Peel away foil cups carefully (or dip molds in warm water 2 to 5 seconds to unmold).
  Makes 2¾ cups or 6 servings

Variations: Substitute 1 can (16 ounces) drained fruit cocktail OR 1 can (17 ounces) drained and finely chopped sliced peaches OR 1½ cups finely chopped fresh fruit or vegetables for the orange and carrot. For the canned fruits, use those packed in water or unsweetened fruit juice.

Nutrition Information Per Serving:			
Calories	18	Fat	0 g
Cholesterol	0 mg	Carbohydrate	3 g
Sodium	45 mg	Protein	1 g

Diabetic Exchanges Per Serving:
Free, Limited

Citrus Sensation

1 package (4-serving size) JELL-O Brand Lemon, Lime or Orange Flavor Sugar Free Gelatin
¾ cup boiling water
½ cup cold water
 Ice cubes
½ cup lemon sherbet

- Completely dissolve gelatin in boiling water; pour into blender container.

- Combine cold water and enough ice cubes to measure 1¼ cups. Add to gelatin; stir until ice is partially melted. Add sherbet; cover. Blend at high speed 30 seconds. Spoon into individual dishes or medium serving bowl. Chill until set, about 45 minutes.
  Makes 3 cups or 6 servings

Nutrition Information Per Serving:			
Calories	30	Fat	0 g
Cholesterol	0 mg	Carbohydrate	5 g
Sodium	50 mg	Protein	1 g

Diabetic Exchanges Per Serving:
½ Starch

Fresh Fruit Parfaits

This recipe offers several delicious variations. (The nutrition information applies to the ingredients listed in the recipe.)

1/2 **cup blueberries**
1/2 **cup sliced strawberries**
1 **package (4-serving size) JELL-O Brand Sugar Free Gelatin, any flavor**
3/4 **cup boiling water**
1/2 **cup cold water**
   Ice cubes
3/4 **cup thawed COOL WHIP LITE Whipped Topping**

- Divide fruit among 6 parfait glasses. Completely dissolve gelatin in boiling water. Combine cold water and enough ice cubes to measure 1 1/4 cups. Add to gelatin; stir until slightly thickened. Remove any unmelted ice. Measure 3/4 cup gelatin; pour 2 tablespoons into each glass. Chill until set but not firm.

- Gently stir whipped topping into remaining gelatin. Spoon over fruit in glasses. Chill until set, about 1 hour.

Makes about 3 cups or 6 servings

Suggested combinations:
- Orange flavor gelatin and 1 cup peach slices.

- Lime flavor gelatin and 1 cup cantaloupe balls *or* 1 medium banana, sliced.

- Strawberry flavor gelatin and 1 cup strawberry slices *or* 1 medium banana, sliced.

- Lemon flavor gelatin and 1 cup red seedless grapes.

Nutrition Information Per Serving:			
Calories	35	Fat	1 g
Cholesterol	0 mg	Carbohydrate	5 g
Sodium	50 mg	Protein	1 g

Diabetic Exchanges Per Serving:
1/2 Fruit

Quick Berry Parfaits

This dessert "magically" forms layers!

1 **package (4-serving size) JELL-O Brand Sugar Free Gelatin, any red flavor**
3/4 **cup boiling water**
1/2 **cup cold cranberry juice**
   Ice cubes
1/2 **cup thawed COOL WHIP LITE Whipped Topping**

- Completely dissolve gelatin in boiling water; pour into blender container. Combine cranberry juice and enough ice cubes to measure 1 1/4 cups. Add to gelatin; stir until ice is partially melted. Cover; blend at high speed 10 seconds. Add whipped topping; cover. Blend 15 seconds. Pour half of the gelatin mixture into 6 straight-sided dessert glasses; let stand 1 minute. Top with remaining gelatin mixture. Chill until set, about 1 hour. Garnish if desired.

Makes 6 servings

Nutrition Information Per Serving:			
Calories	30	Fat	1 g
Cholesterol	0 mg	Carbohydrate	5 g
Sodium	45 mg	Protein	1 g

Diabetic Exchanges Per Serving:
1/2 Fruit

Quick Berry Parfaits

Fruit Sparkles

The nutrition information applies to the ingredients listed in the recipe.

- **1 package (4-serving size) JELL-O Brand Sugar Free Gelatin, any flavor**
- **1 cup boiling water**
- **1 cup chilled fruit-flavored seltzer, sparkling water, club soda or other sugar free carbonated beverage**
- **1 cup combined sliced bananas and strawberries**

- Completely dissolve gelatin in boiling water. Add beverage. Chill until slightly thickened. Stir in fruit. Pour into individual dishes or medium serving bowl. Chill until firm, about 1 hour. Garnish if desired.

Makes 3 cups or 6 servings

Suggested Combinations:
- Lime flavor gelatin and 1 can (8 ounces) pear halves in juice, drained.

- Raspberry flavor gelatin and 1 can (8 ounces) fruit cocktail in juice *or* sliced peaches in juice, drained.

- Cherry flavor gelatin and 1 medium banana, sliced.

- Strawberry flavor gelatin and 1 cup sliced strawberries.

- Orange flavor gelatin and 1 cup drained mandarin orange sections *or* unsweetened crushed pineapple.

Nutrition Information Per Serving:

Calories	25	Fat	0 g
Cholesterol	0 mg	Carbohydrate	5 g
Sodium	50 mg	Protein	1 g

Diabetic Exchanges Per Serving:
½ Fruit

Fruited Gelatin and Cottage Cheese

- **1 container (16 ounces) 4% fat cottage cheese**
- **1 package (4-serving size) JELL-O Brand Orange Flavor Sugar Free Gelatin**
- **¾ cup boiling water**
- **½ cup cold water Ice cubes**
- **1 can (11 ounces) mandarin orange sections, drained**

- Place cottage cheese in blender or food processor container; cover. Blend until smooth; set aside.

- Completely dissolve gelatin in boiling water. Combine cold water and enough ice cubes to measure 1¼ cups. Add to gelatin; stir until slightly thickened. Remove any unmelted ice; stir in oranges. Divide cottage cheese among 8 individual serving dishes. Spoon gelatin mixture over cottage cheese. Chill until set, about 2 hours.

Makes about 4 cups or 8 servings

Nutrition Information Per Serving:

Calories	80	Fat	3 g
Cholesterol	10 mg	Carbohydrate	5 g
Sodium	260 mg	Protein	8 g

Diabetic Exchanges Per Serving:
1 Lean Meat, ½ Fruit

Fruit Sparkles

Creamy Yogurt Cups

For extra flavor, substitute ¹/₂ cup fruit juice for the cold water. (This will slightly increase the calorie count.)

1 package (4-serving size) JELL-O Brand Sugar Free Gelatin, any flavor
³/₄ cup boiling water
¹/₂ cup cold water
    Ice cubes
1 container (8 ounces) vanilla lowfat yogurt
¹/₂ teaspoon vanilla (optional)

• Completely dissolve gelatin in boiling water. Combine cold water and enough ice cubes to measure 1 cup. Add to gelatin; stir until slightly thickened. Remove any unmelted ice. Stir in yogurt and vanilla. Pour into 5 individual dishes. Chill until set, about 30 minutes. Garnish if desired.

Makes 2¹/₂ cups or 5 servings

Nutrition Information Per Serving:

Calories	50	Fat	1 g
Cholesterol	5 mg	Carbohydrate	7 g
Sodium	85 mg	Protein	4 g

Diabetic Exchanges Per Serving:
¹/₂ Nonfat Milk

JELL-O JIGGLERS
Gelatin Snacks

This reduced-calorie version of our extremely popular children's snack makes a great eat-on-the-run treat.

1 package (4-serving size) JELL-O Brand Gelatin, any flavor
1 package (4-serving size) JELL-O Brand Sugar Free Gelatin, any flavor (same flavor as regular gelatin)
1¹/₄ cups boiling water

• Completely dissolve gelatin in boiling water. Pour into 8- or 9-inch square pan. Chill until firm, about 3 hours. Cut into 1¹/₂-inch squares.

Makes 3 dozen JELL-O JIGGLERS

Nutrition Information Per Serving (1 square):

Calories	10	Fat	0 g
Cholesterol	0 mg	Carbohydrate	2 g
Sodium	15 mg	Protein	0 g

Diabetic Exchanges Per Serving:
Free, Limited

JELL-O JIGGLERS Yogurt Snacks:
Dissolve gelatin in boiling water as directed. Cool to room temperature. Whisk in 1 container (8 ounces) plain lowfat yogurt. Continue as directed.

Nutrition Information Per Serving (1 square):

Calories	14	Fat	0 g
Cholesterol	0 mg	Carbohydrate	3 g
Sodium	20 mg	Protein	1 g

Diabetic Exchanges Per Serving:
Free, Limited

Creamy Yogurt Cups

Sparkling Lemon Ice

We garnished this frosty dessert with fresh raspberries and mint leaves.

1 package (4-serving size) JELL-O Brand Lemon Flavor Sugar Free Gelatin
1 cup boiling water
1 cup cold lemon-lime seltzer
3 tablespoons fresh lemon juice
½ teaspoon grated lemon peel

- Completely dissolve gelatin in boiling water. Add seltzer, lemon juice and peel. Pour into 8- or 9-inch square pan; cover. Freeze until firm, about 3 hours.

- Remove from freezer; let stand at room temperature 10 minutes to soften slightly. Beat at medium speed with electric mixer or process with food processor until smooth. Spoon or scoop into individual dishes. Serve immediately.

Makes 6 servings

Nutrition Information Per Serving:

Calories	8	Fat	0 g
Cholesterol	0 mg	Carbohydrate	1 g
Sodium	50 mg	Protein	1 g

Diabetic Exchanges Per Serving:
Free

Cherry Almond Supreme

1 can (8 ounces) pitted dark sweet cherries in light syrup, undrained
1 package (4-serving size) JELL-O Brand Cherry Flavor Sugar Free Gelatin
¾ cup boiling water
Ice cubes
2 tablespoons chopped toasted almonds
1 cup thawed COOL WHIP LITE Whipped Topping

- Drain cherries, reserving syrup. If necessary, add enough water to reserved syrup to measure ½ cup. Cut cherries into quarters.

- Completely dissolve gelatin in boiling water. Combine measured syrup and enough ice to measure 1¼ cups. Add to gelatin; stir until slightly thickened. Remove any unmelted ice. Chill until thickened. Measure 1¼ cups gelatin; stir in half of the cherries and nuts. Set aside.

- Gently stir whipped topping into remaining gelatin. Add the remaining cherries and nuts; spoon into 6 dessert glasses. Chill until set but not firm, about 15 minutes. Top with clear gelatin mixture. Chill until set, about 1 hour.

Makes about 3 cups or 6 servings

Nutrition Information Per Serving:

Calories	70	Fat	3 g
Cholesterol	0 mg	Carbohydrate	10 g
Sodium	65 mg	Protein	2 g

Diabetic Exchanges Per Serving:
1 Fruit, ½ Fat

Sparkling Lemon Ice

Applesauce Snack Cups

Applesauce adds special flavor to this recipe. Double this recipe for some extras to have on hand.

1 package (4-serving size) JELL-O Brand Sugar Free Gelatin, any red flavor
1 cup boiling water
¾ cup cold unsweetened applesauce
¼ teaspoon ground cinnamon
½ cup vanilla lowfat yogurt

- Completely dissolve gelatin in boiling water. Measure ¾ cup gelatin; combine with applesauce and cinnamon. Pour into 4 individual dishes or medium serving bowl. Chill until set but not firm.

- Chill remaining gelatin until slightly thickened. Stir in yogurt until well blended; spoon over gelatin in dishes. Chill until set, about 2 hours. Garnish if desired.

Makes 2 cups or 4 servings

Nutrition Information Per Serving:

Calories	60	Fat	0 g
Cholesterol	0 mg	Carbohydrate	10 g
Sodium	85 mg	Protein	3 g

Diabetic Exchanges Per Serving:
1 Fruit

Ambrosia Parfaits

This heavenly dessert is aptly named. In Greek and Roman mythology, ambrosia was a food of the gods.

1 can (8 ounces) pineapple tidbits *or* crushed pineapple in unsweetened pineapple juice, undrained
1½ cups cold 2% lowfat milk
1 package (4-serving size) JELL-O Vanilla Flavor Sugar Free Instant Pudding and Pie Filling
1 small banana, chopped
1 cup sliced strawberries
¼ cup BAKER'S ANGEL FLAKE Coconut, toasted

- Drain pineapple, reserving juice. Pour reserved juice and milk into medium mixing bowl. Add pudding mix. Beat with wire whisk until well blended, 1 to 2 minutes. Stir in banana.

- Spoon half of the pudding mixture into parfait glasses; cover with a layer of strawberries, pineapple and coconut. Top with remaining pudding mixture. Refrigerate until ready to serve.

Makes 6 servings

Nutrition Information Per Serving:

Calories	110	Fat	2 g
Cholesterol	5 mg	Carbohydrate	19 g
Sodium	260 mg	Protein	3 g

Diabetic Exchanges Per Serving:
1½ Fruit, ½ Fat

Applesauce Snack Cups

CHOCOLATE INDULGENCES

Surprised to find an entire chapter of chocolate recipes in a cookbook devoted to lower-calorie recipes? Totally eliminating treat foods like chocolate just because you are watching your weight can leave you feeling deprived and cause you to fall off the dieting bandwagon.

With the help of Sugar Free JELL-O Brand Pudding, you can include luscious chocolate desserts in your diet. If you are longing for the wickedly decadent flavor combination of chocolate and peanut butter, and think it's a "no-no" on a diet, the recipe for Chocolate Peanut Butter Parfaits at 110 calories per serving is sure to fulfill your fantasy. And, if chocolate mousse is a must, you're sure to be impressed with our heavenly version of this dessert classic. If you're looking for comfort, and chocolate is your solution, our Chocolate Bread Pudding could prove to be the *ultimate* comfort food.

Page through this chapter for all kinds of divine ways to *sensibly* indulge in chocolate.

Black Forest Parfaits (page 32)

Black Forest Parfaits

Yummm! Layers of chocolate cake, cherries and chocolate mousse form a chocolate lover's dream dessert.

2 cups cold 2% lowfat milk, divided
4 ounces neufchatel cheese
1 package (4-serving size) JELL-O Chocolate Flavor Sugar Free Instant Pudding and Pie Filling
1 package (15 ounces) ENTENMANN'S Fat Free Chocolate Loaf, cubed
1 can (20 ounces) reduced-calorie cherry pie filling
1 square (1 ounce) BAKER'S Semi-Sweet Chocolate, grated (page 62)

- Pour ½ cup of the milk into blender container. Add neufchatel cheese; cover. Blend until smooth. Add the remaining 1½ cups milk and the pudding mix; cover. Blend until smooth.

- Divide cake cubes evenly among 12 individual dishes. Reserve a few cherries for garnish if desired; spoon remaining cherry pie filling over cake cubes. Top with pudding mixture. Refrigerate until ready to serve. Top with reserved cherries and chocolate.
    Makes 12 servings

Nutrition Information Per Serving:			
Calories	190	Fat	4 g
Cholesterol	10 mg	Carbohydrate	36 g
Sodium	340 mg	Protein	4 g

Diabetic Exchanges Per Serving:
1½ Fruit*, 1 Starch, 1 Fat

*A fruit exchange is used to describe this recipe since most of its carbohydrate value comes from simple sugars. However, this recipe is not the nutritional equivalent of a fruit.

Chocolate Peanut Butter Parfaits

This favorite American flavor combination is captured sublimely in this creamy dessert.

2 cups plus 2 tablespoons cold skim milk, divided
2 tablespoons chunky peanut butter
1 cup thawed COOL WHIP LITE Whipped Topping
1 package (4-serving size) JELL-O Chocolate Flavor Sugar Free Instant Pudding and Pie Filling

- Add 2 tablespoons of the milk to the peanut butter; stir until well blended. Stir in whipped topping.

- Pour the remaining 2 cups milk into medium mixing bowl. Add pudding mix. Beat with wire whisk until well blended, 1 to 2 minutes. Spoon half of the pudding mixture into 6 parfait glasses; cover with whipped topping mixture. Top with the remaining pudding mixture. Refrigerate until ready to serve.
    Makes 3 cups or 6 servings

Nutrition Information Per Serving:			
Calories	110	Fat	5 g
Cholesterol	0 mg	Carbohydrate	13 g
Sodium	290 mg	Protein	5 g

Diabetic Exchanges Per Serving:
1 Starch, 1 Fat

Chocolate Peanut Butter Parfaits

Chocolate Bread Pudding

4 slices firm-textured white bread
2 teaspoons margarine, melted
¼ cup BAKER'S Semi-Sweet Real Chocolate Chips
2 cups cold 2% lowfat milk
½ cup thawed frozen egg substitute
1 teaspoon vanilla
1 package (4-serving size) JELL-O Chocolate Flavor Sugar Free Pudding and Pie Filling

• Heat oven to 350°F.

• Lightly brush both sides of bread slices with margarine. Cut into ½-inch cubes. Place on cookie sheet. Bake 10 minutes or until lightly toasted. Place in 8-inch square pan; sprinkle with chocolate chips.

• Pour milk, egg substitute and vanilla into large mixing bowl. Beat with wire whisk until well blended. Add pudding mix; whisk until well blended, 1 to 2 minutes. Pour over bread cubes in pan. Bake 30 minutes. Remove from oven; let stand 10 minutes before serving.

Makes 8 servings

Nutrition Information Per Serving:
Calories 120 Fat 4 g
Cholesterol 5 mg Carbohydrate 16 g
Sodium 170 mg Protein 5 g

Diabetic Exchanges Per Serving:
1 Starch, 1 Fat

Chocolate Raspberry Cheesecake

Freeze a single slice for when chocolate attacks hit.

¾ cup cold skim milk
1 cup 1% lowfat cottage cheese
⅓ cup seedless raspberry fruit spread
1 package (4-serving size) JELL-O Chocolate Flavor Sugar Free Instant Pudding and Pie Filling
2 cups thawed COOL WHIP LITE Whipped Topping
1 square (1 ounce) BAKER'S Semi-Sweet Chocolate, grated (page 62)
½ cup raspberries

• Pour milk into blender container. Add cottage cheese and fruit spread; cover. Blend until smooth. Add pudding mix; cover. Blend until smooth.

• Pour pudding mixture into large bowl; gently stir in whipped topping. Pour into 8-inch pie plate; smooth top. Sprinkle with chocolate. Freeze until firm, 6 hours or overnight.

• Remove cheesecake from freezer about 15 minutes before serving. Let stand at room temperature to soften slightly. Top with raspberries.

Makes 8 servings

Nutrition Information Per Serving:
Calories 120 Fat 4 g
Cholesterol 0 mg Carbohydrate 16 g
Sodium 310 mg Protein 5 g

Diabetic Exchanges Per Serving:
½ Medium Fat Meat, 1 Starch

Chocolate Cookie Crumble

Crumbled chocolate wafers add textural contrast to this satisfying layered dessert. To treat yourself extra special, serve it in a stemmed wine glass.

2 cups cold skim milk, divided
4 ounces pasteurized process cream cheese product
1 package (4-serving size) JELL-O Chocolate Flavor Sugar Free Instant Pudding and Pie Filling
6 chocolate wafer cookies, crumbled

- Pour ½ cup of the milk into blender container. Add cream cheese product; cover. Blend until smooth. Add the remaining 1½ cups milk and the pudding mix; cover. Blend until smooth. Spoon half of the pudding mixture into 6 individual dishes; cover with crumbled cookies. Top with the remaining pudding mixture. Refrigerate until ready to serve.

Makes 6 servings

Nutrition Information Per Serving:

Calories	120	Fat	5 g
Cholesterol	10 mg	Carbohydrate	15 g
Sodium	410 mg	Protein	6 g

Diabetic Exchanges Per Serving:
½ Whole Milk, ½ Starch

Chocolate Pudding Sandwiches

If the filling mixture softens while you are preparing the sandwiches, return it to the refrigerator for a few minutes.

1½ cups cold skim milk
1 package (4-serving size) JELL-O Chocolate Flavor Sugar Free Instant Pudding and Pie Filling
3¼ cups (8 ounces) COOL WHIP LITE Whipped Topping, thawed
1 cup miniature marshmallows
1 package (9 ounces) chocolate wafer cookies (44 cookies)

- Pour milk into large mixing bowl. Add pudding mix. Beat with wire whisk until well blended, 1 to 2 minutes. Gently stir in whipped topping and marshmallows.

- For each sandwich, spread about 2 tablespoons of the pudding mixture onto each of 2 cookies. Lightly press cookies together to form sandwich. Wrap each sandwich with plastic wrap. Repeat with remaining cookies and pudding mixture. Freeze until firm, about 6 hours or overnight.

- Remove sandwiches from freezer about 5 minutes before serving. Let stand at room temperature to soften slightly.

Makes 22 sandwiches

Nutrition Information Per Serving (1 sandwich):

Calories	100	Fat	3 g
Cholesterol	0 mg	Carbohydrate	16 g
Sodium	170 mg	Protein	2 g

Diabetic Information Per Serving:
1 Starch, 1 Fat

Vanilla Pudding Grahamwiches

These are great to have on hand for a quick snack.

1½ cups cold skim milk
1 package (4-serving size) JELL-O Vanilla Flavor Sugar Free Instant Pudding and Pie Filling
3¼ cups (8 ounces) COOL WHIP LITE Whipped Topping, thawed
1 cup miniature marshmallows
22 whole cinnamon graham crackers, broken into 44 squares
2 squares (2 ounces) BAKER'S Semi-Sweet Chocolate, grated (page 62)

• Pour milk into large mixing bowl. Add pudding mix. Beat with wire whisk until well blended, 1 to 2 minutes. Gently stir in whipped topping and marshmallows.

• For each sandwich, spread about 2 tablespoons of the pudding mixture onto each of 2 graham cracker squares. Lightly press graham crackers together to form sandwich. Repeat with the remaining graham crackers and pudding mixture. Press edges of each sandwich into chocolate to coat. Wrap each sandwich with plastic wrap. Freeze until firm, about 6 hours or overnight.

• Remove grahamwiches from freezer about 5 minutes before serving. Let stand at room temperature to soften slightly.
Makes 22 sandwiches

Note: Store any leftover sandwiches in freezer in plastic bag or airtight container.

Nutrition Information Per Serving (1 sandwich):			
Calories	120	Fat	4 g
Cholesterol	0 mg	Carbohydrate	20 g
Sodium	140 mg	Protein	4 g

Diabetic Exchanges Per Serving:
1 Starch, 1 Fat

Chocolate Banana Pops

2 cups cold skim milk
1 package (4-serving size) JELL-O Chocolate Flavor Sugar Free Instant Pudding and Pie Filling
1 cup thawed COOL WHIP LITE Whipped Topping
½ cup mashed banana

• Pour milk into medium mixing bowl. Add pudding mix. Beat with wire whisk until well blended, 1 to 2 minutes. Gently stir in whipped topping and banana. Spoon about ⅓ cup pudding mixture into each of ten (5-ounce) paper cups. Insert wooden stick or plastic spoon into each for handle. Freeze until firm, about 5 hours. To serve, press firmly on bottom of cup to release pop.
Makes 10 pops

Nutrition Information Per Serving (1 pop):			
Calories	60	Fat	1 g
Cholesterol	0 mg	Carbohydrate	10 g
Sodium	160 mg	Protein	2 g

Diabetic Exchanges Per Serving:
1 Starch

Left to right: Chocolate Pudding Sandwiches (page 35); Vanilla Pudding Grahamwiches

Mocha-Spice Dessert

2 cups cold skim milk
1 package (4-serving size)
    JELL-O Chocolate Flavor
    Sugar Free Instant Pudding
    and Pie Filling
1 tablespoon MAXWELL HOUSE
    or YUBAN Instant Coffee or
    SANKA Brand 99.7%
    Caffeine Free Instant Coffee
1½ cups thawed COOL WHIP LITE
    Whipped Topping
¼ teaspoon ground cinnamon

- Pour milk into large mixing bowl.
  Add pudding mix and instant
  coffee. Beat with wire whisk until
  well blended, 1 to 2 minutes.
  Pour into medium serving bowl
  or individual dishes. Refrigerate.

- Just before serving, combine
  whipped topping and cinnamon;
  spread over pudding. Garnish if
  desired.

    Makes 6 servings

Nutrition Information Per Serving:

Calories	90	Fat	3 g
Cholesterol	0 mg	Carbohydrate	13 g
Sodium	270 mg	Protein	4 g

Diabetic Information Per Serving:
½ 2% Lowfat Milk, ½ Starch

Chocolate Mousse

*You'll never believe this luscious
mousse contains 90 calories per
serving. It's also great when made
with the other flavors of JELL-O
Sugar Free Instant Pudding. Top it
with a tablespoon of COOL WHIP
LITE Whipped Topping for 8 extra
calories and a little treat.*

1½ cups cold skim milk
1 package (4-serving size)
    JELL-O Chocolate Flavor
    Sugar Free Instant Pudding
    and Pie Filling
1 cup thawed COOL WHIP LITE
    Whipped Topping
¼ cup raspberries

- Pour milk into medium mixing
  bowl. Add pudding mix. Beat with
  wire whisk until well blended, 1 to
  2 minutes. Gently stir in whipped
  topping. Spoon into individual
  dishes or medium serving bowl.
  Refrigerate until ready to serve.
  Top with raspberries. Garnish if
  desired.
    Makes 2⅔ cups or 5 servings

Nutrition Information Per Serving:

Calories	90	Fat	2 g
Cholesterol	0 mg	Carbohydrate	13 g
Sodium	310 mg	Protein	4 g

Diabetic Exchanges Per Serving:
½ 2% Lowfat Milk, ½ Starch

Top to bottom: Mocha-Spice Dessert;
Chocolate Mousse

SWEET &
SAVORY SALADS

Salads are a dieter's mainstay and JELL-O Brand Gelatin has long been a favorite salad ingredient. With Sugar Free JELL-O as a base, the wholesome salads featured in this chapter are FAT FREE!!! Some of these recipes are classic JELL-O Gelatin salads that have been adapted to fit today's healthier lifestyle and others are brand new creations from the Test Kitchens at General Foods.

Most of the salads are packed with fruits and vegetables. In many cases, you can even double up on portions and still come out with a salad containing less than 100 calories. Try colorful and refreshing Three Pepper Salad at only 16 calories per serving, Sunset Yogurt Salad at only 40 calories per serving or Gazpacho Salad at only 25 calories per serving, for starters.

Make up individual portions of any one of these salads for a cool and colorful addition to any family meal. Save any leftovers for a delicious low-calorie snack.

Turn the page for some super solutions for adding a side dish to fill out a meal without filling out your waistband.

Sparkling Berry Salad (page 42)

Sparkling Berry Salad

*The nutrition information applies
to the ingredients listed in the
recipe.*

  2 cups cranberry juice
  2 packages (4-serving size
      each) or 1 package
      (8-serving size) JELL-O
      Brand Sugar Free Gelatin,
      any red flavor
1½ cups cold club soda
  ¼ cup creme de cassis liqueur
  1 teaspoon lemon juice
  1 cup raspberries
  1 cup blueberries
  ½ cup sliced strawberries
  ½ cup whole strawberries, cut
      into fans

• Bring cranberry juice to a boil in
  medium saucepan. Completely
  dissolve gelatin in boiling
  cranberry juice. Stir in club soda,
  liqueur and lemon juice. Chill until
  slightly thickened.

• Reserve a few raspberries and
  blueberries for garnish, if
  desired. Stir remaining
  raspberries, blueberries and the
  sliced strawberries into gelatin
  mixture. Spoon into 6-cup mold
  which has been lightly sprayed
  with non-stick cooking spray.
  Chill until firm, about 4 hours.
  Unmold. Surround with reserved
  berries and the strawberry fans.
                    Makes 8 servings

Variation: Omit creme de cassis
liqueur. Increase cranberry juice to
2¼ cups.

Nutrition Information Per Serving:
Calories   100 Fat   0 g
Cholesterol 0 mg Carbohydrate 18 g
Sodium   85 mg Protein   2 g

Diabetic Exchanges Per Serving:
1½ Fruit

Gazpacho Salad

*This salad is also great served
molded. Just make sure to spray
molds with non-stick cooking spray.*

1½ cups tomato juice
  1 package (4-serving size)
      JELL-O Brand Lemon Flavor
      Sugar Free Gelatin
  1 cup finely chopped tomato
  ½ cup finely chopped peeled
      cucumber
  ¼ cup finely chopped green
      pepper
  2 tablespoons finely chopped
      red pepper
  2 tablespoons sliced green
      onions
  2 tablespoons vinegar
  ¼ teaspoon black pepper
  ⅛ teaspoon garlic powder
      (optional)

• Bring tomato juice to a boil in
  small saucepan. Completely
  dissolve gelatin in boiling tomato
  juice. Chill until slightly thickened.

• Combine remaining ingredients
  in medium bowl; mix well. Stir
  into gelatin mixture. Pour into
  individual dishes or medium
  serving bowl. Chill until firm,
  about 3 hours.
          Makes 3⅔ cups or 7 servings

Nutrition Information Per Serving:
Calories   25 Fat   0 g
Cholesterol 0 mg Carbohydrate   4 g
Sodium   220 mg Protein   2 g

Diabetic Exchanges Per Serving:
1 Vegetable

Gazpacho Salad

SWEET & SAVORY SALADS

Three Pepper Salad

Peppers add a generous supply of Vitamin C to this festive salad.

2 packages (4-serving size each) or 1 package (8-serving size) JELL-O Brand Lemon Flavor Sugar Free Gelatin
2 cups boiling water
1½ cups cold water
2 tablespoons lemon juice
2 cups chopped red, green and/or yellow peppers
2 tablespoons sliced green onions

- Completely dissolve gelatin in boiling water. Stir in cold water and lemon juice. Chill until slightly thickened.

- Stir in peppers and green onions. Pour into 5-cup mold which has been lightly sprayed with non-stick cooking spray. Chill until firm, about 4 hours. Unmold.

Makes 10 servings

Nutrition Information Per Serving:			
Calories	16	Fat	0 g
Cholesterol	0 mg	Carbohydrate	2 g
Sodium	50 mg	Protein	1 g

Diabetic Exchanges Per Serving:
Free, Limited

Carrot Raisin Salad

Use either dark or golden raisins. This salad supplies over 75% of the U.S. RDA for Vitamin A.

1 package (4-serving size) JELL-O Brand Orange Flavor Sugar Free Gelatin
¾ cup boiling water
2 tablespoons raisins
½ cup cold orange juice
Ice cubes
½ cup shredded carrot

- Completely dissolve gelatin in boiling water. Stir in raisins. Combine juice and enough ice cubes to measure 1¼ cups. Add to gelatin; stir until slightly thickened. Remove any unmelted ice. Stir in carrot. Spoon into individual dishes or small serving bowl. Chill until firm, about 2 hours.

Makes 2 cups or 4 servings

Nutrition Information Per Serving:			
Calories	40	Fat	0 g
Cholesterol	0 mg	Carbohydrate	8 g
Sodium	65 mg	Protein	2 g

Diabetic Exchanges Per Serving:
½ Fruit

Three Pepper Salad

Sunset Yogurt Salad

Shredded carrots and crushed pineapple add flavor to this two-layered mold, which contains over 50% of the U.S. RDA for Vitamin A.

2 packages (4-serving size each) or 1 package (8-serving size) JELL-O Brand Orange or Lemon Flavor Sugar Free Gelatin
2 cups boiling water
1 container (8 ounces) plain lowfat yogurt
¼ cup cold water
1 can (8 ounces) crushed pineapple in unsweetened juice, undrained
1 cup shredded carrots

• Completely dissolve gelatin in boiling water. Measure 1 cup gelatin into medium mixing bowl; chill until slightly thickened. Stir in yogurt. Pour into medium serving bowl. Chill until set but not firm.

• Add cold water to the remaining gelatin. Stir in pineapple and carrots. Chill until slightly thickened. Spoon over gelatin-yogurt mixture in bowl. Chill until firm, about 4 hours. Garnish if desired.

Makes 5 cups or 10 servings

Nutrition Information Per Serving:

Calories	40	Fat	0 g
Cholesterol	0 mg	Carbohydrate	7 g
Sodium	65 mg	Protein	3 g

Diabetic Exchanges Per Serving:
½ Starch

Orange Onion Salad

1 package (4-serving size) JELL-O Brand Orange Flavor Sugar Free Gelatin
¾ cup boiling water
1 tablespoon vinegar
Dash of white pepper
½ cup cold water
Ice cubes
2 oranges, peeled, sectioned and drained (about 1 cup)
¼ cup chopped celery
1 to 2 tablespoons chopped red onion

• Completely dissolve gelatin in boiling water. Add vinegar and pepper. Combine cold water and enough ice cubes to measure 1¼ cups. Add to gelatin; stir until slightly thickened. Remove any unmelted ice. Add oranges, celery and onion. Spoon into individual dishes or medium serving bowl. Chill until firm, about 2 hours.

Makes 6 servings

Nutrition Information Per Serving:

Calories	30	Fat	0 g
Cholesterol	0 mg	Carbohydrate	6 g
Sodium	40 mg	Protein	1 g

Diabetic Exchanges Per Serving:
½ Fruit

Sunset Yogurt Salad

White Sangria Splash

Wine adds a spirited touch to this festive salad. If you'd prefer, substitute fruit juice for the wine. This salad is also good when made with orange segments and chopped apple. (The nutrition information applies to the ingredients listed in the recipe.)

1½ cups dry white wine
2 packages (4-serving size each) or 1 package (8-serving size) JELL-O Brand Lemon Flavor Sugar Free Gelatin
2½ cups cold club soda
1 tablespoon lime juice
1 tablespoon orange liqueur (optional)
1 cup sliced strawberries
1 cup seedless red grapes
1 cup seedless green grapes

- Bring wine to a boil in small saucepan. Completely dissolve gelatin in the boiling wine; pour into medium bowl. Stir in club soda, lime juice and liqueur. Place bowl in larger bowl of ice and water; let stand about 10 minutes until slightly thickened, stirring occasionally.

- Stir in fruit. Pour into 6-cup mold which has been lightly sprayed with non-stick cooking spray. Chill until firm, about 4 hours. Unmold. Serve with additional fruit, if desired.
    Makes 6 cups or 12 servings

Nutrition Information Per Serving:			
Calories	50	Fat	0 g
Cholesterol	0 mg	Carbohydrate	7 g
Sodium	55 mg	Protein	1 g

Diabetic Exchanges Per Serving:
1 Fruit

Cherry Waldorf Salad

1¼ cups apple juice, divided
1 package (4-serving size) JELL-O Brand Cherry Flavor Sugar Free Gelatin
Ice cubes
½ cup finely chopped peeled apple
1 small banana, sliced or finely chopped
¼ cup sliced celery

- Bring ¾ cup of the apple juice to a boil in medium saucepan. Completely dissolve gelatin in boiling apple juice. Combine the remaining ½ cup apple juice and enough ice cubes to measure 1¼ cups. Add to gelatin; stir until slightly thickened. Remove any unmelted ice. Stir in fruit and celery. Spoon into individual dishes or medium serving bowl. Chill until firm, about 2 hours.
    Makes 2½ cups or 5 servings

Nutrition Information Per Serving:			
Calories	60	Fat	0 g
Cholesterol	0 mg	Carbohydrate	13 g
Sodium	55 mg	Protein	1 g

Diabetic Exchanges Per Serving:
1 Fruit

White Sangria Splash

LUNCH IN A CUP

One of the biggest challenges dieters face is to eat only a controlled portion of food. With the help of Sugar Free JELL-O Brand Gelatin, lunch salads take on a whole new dimension.

All of the make-ahead recipes in this chapter can stand on their own as a substantial lunch entree. Each of these recipes contains no more than 160 calories per serving. You'll want to add variety to your diet by adding other accompaniments such as a whole-grain roll, a glass of skim milk or lowfat yogurt, and vegetables and/or fruit. Prepare them in individual plastic containers with tight-fitting lids, pack them in an insulated lunch bag and you are ready to go. Make dieting easier by taking turns preparing these lunches with a partner.

Of course, you won't have to save these salads just for lunch. When you are ravenous after a late day, any one of the following recipes would make a perfect solution for a satisfying supper entree.

Chef's Salad (page 52)

Chef's Salad

*To julienne turkey and cheese, cut
into matchstick-size pieces.*

- **1 package (4-serving size)
  JELL-O Brand Lemon Flavor
  Sugar Free Gelatin**
- **¼ teaspoon salt**
- **¾ cup boiling water**
- **½ cup cold water
  Ice cubes**
- **1 tablespoon vinegar**
- **2 teaspoons reduced-calorie
  French dressing**
- **¼ teaspoon Worcestershire
  sauce**
- **⅛ teaspoon white pepper**
- **¾ cup chopped tomato**
- **½ cup finely shredded lettuce**
- **½ cup julienned cooked turkey
  breast**
- **½ cup julienned Swiss cheese**
- **2 tablespoons sliced green
  onions**
- **2 tablespoons quartered radish
  slices**

- Completely dissolve gelatin and
  salt in boiling water. Combine
  cold water and enough ice cubes
  to measure 1¼ cups. Add to
  gelatin; stir until slightly
  thickened. Remove any unmelted
  ice. Stir in vinegar, dressing,
  Worcestershire sauce and
  pepper. Chill until slightly
  thickened.

- Stir remaining ingredients into
  gelatin mixture. Spoon into 3
  individual plastic containers or

serving dishes. Chill until firm,
about 2 hours. Garnish if desired.

*Makes 3½ cups or
3 entree servings*

Nutrition Information Per Serving:

Calories	100	Fat	4 g
Cholesterol	30 mg	Carbohydrate	4 g
Sodium	330 mg	Protein	12 g

Diabetic Exchanges Per Serving:
1 Medium Fat Meat, 1 Vegetable

Taco Salad

- **2 packages (4-serving size
  each) or 1 package
  (8-serving size) JELL-O
  Brand Lemon Flavor Sugar
  Free Gelatin**
- **2 cups boiling water**
- **1 cup frozen corn**
- **1 cup drained canned kidney
  beans**
- **½ cup medium salsa**
- **¼ cup (1 ounce) shredded
  cheddar cheese**
- **2 tablespoons vinegar**
- **½ teaspoon chili powder**

- Completely dissolve gelatin in
  boiling water. Chill until slightly
  thickened. Stir in remaining
  ingredients. Spoon gelatin
  mixture into 4 individual plastic
  containers or serving dishes.
  Chill until firm, about 2 hours.

*Makes 5 cups or
4 entree servings*

Nutrition Information Per Serving:

Calories	140	Fat	4 g
Cholesterol	10 mg	Carbohydrate	19 g
Sodium	560 mg	Protein	10 g

Diabetic Exchanges Per Serving:
½ Medium Fat Meat, 1½ Starch

Dijon Chicken Salad

1 cup low-sodium chicken broth
1 package (4-serving size)
    JELL-O Brand Lemon Flavor
    Sugar Free Gelatin
¾ cup cold water
1 tablespoon vinegar
¼ teaspoon black pepper
¼ cup plain lowfat yogurt
2 tablespoons reduced-calorie
    sour cream
1 tablespoon Dijon-style
    mustard
1 cup finely chopped cooked
    chicken breast
1 cup finely chopped celery
½ cup chopped green or red
    pepper

- Bring chicken broth to a boil in small saucepan. Completely dissolve gelatin in boiling broth. Add water, vinegar and black pepper. Chill until slightly thickened. Stir in yogurt, reduced-calorie sour cream and mustard. Chill until slightly thickened. Stir in remaining ingredients. Spoon into 3 individual plastic containers or serving dishes. Chill until firm, about 2 hours.

*Makes 3¼ cups or
3 entree servings*

Nutrition Information Per Serving:

Calories	160	Fat	6 g
Cholesterol	50 mg	Carbohydrate	6 g
Sodium	460 mg	Protein	19 g

Diabetic Exchanges Per Serving:
2 Lean Meat, 1 Vegetable

Tuna Nicoise

1 can (6½ ounces) tuna packed
    in water, drained and
    coarsely flaked
1 small tomato, finely chopped
    and drained
½ cup cooked cut green beans
2 tablespoons chopped green
    pepper
2 tablespoons chopped red
    onion
2 tablespoons sliced pitted ripe
    olives
2 tablespoons reduced-calorie
    French dressing
1 package (4-serving size)
    JELL-O Brand Lemon Flavor
    Sugar Free Gelatin
1 cup boiling water
½ cup cold water
2 teaspoons vinegar
1 hard-cooked egg

- Combine tuna, vegetables, olives and dressing; mix lightly. Marinate in refrigerator 15 minutes.

- Completely dissolve gelatin in boiling water. Add cold water and vinegar. Chill until slightly thickened.

- Divide tuna mixture among 4 individual plastic containers or serving dishes. Slice egg crosswise into 4 slices; place 1 slice on each serving. Spoon clear gelatin over tops. Chill until firm, about 2 hours.

*Makes 4 cups or
4 entree servings*

Nutrition Information Per Serving:

Calories	100	Fat	3 g
Cholesterol	80 mg	Carbohydrate	4 g
Sodium	340 mg	Protein	14 g

Diabetic Exchanges Per Serving:
2 Lean Meat, 1 Vegetable

Salad Veronique

Garnish individual servings with grapes and celery leaves, if desired.

1 package (4-serving size) JELL-O Brand Lemon Flavor Sugar Free Gelatin
¼ teaspoon salt
1 cup boiling water
¼ teaspoon dried tarragon leaves, crushed (optional)
¾ cup cold water
1 tablespoon lemon juice
1 cup finely chopped cooked turkey breast
½ cup seedless grapes, halved
½ cup finely chopped celery

• Completely dissolve gelatin and salt in boiling water; stir in tarragon. Add cold water and lemon juice. Chill until slightly thickened. Stir in the remaining ingredients. Spoon into 3 individual plastic containers or serving dishes. Chill until firm, about 2 hours.

Makes 3 cups or 3 entree servings

Nutrition Information Per Serving:

Calories	100	Fat	2 g
Cholesterol	35 mg	Carbohydrate	4 g
Sodium	310 mg	Protein	16 g

Diabetic Exchanges Per Serving:
2 Lean Meat, 1 Vegetable

Gingered Pear Salad

Ginger adds a delightful flavor to this salad.

1 can (8½ ounces) pear halves in juice, undrained
1 package (4-serving size) JELL-O Brand Lemon Flavor Sugar Free Gelatin
¾ cup boiling water
2 teaspoons lemon juice
Ice cubes
1 cup (8 ounces) 2% lowfat cottage cheese
⅛ teaspoon salt
⅛ teaspoon ground ginger

• Drain pears, reserving juice; set aside. Finely chop pears; set aside.

• Dissolve gelatin in boiling water; add lemon juice. Add enough ice cubes to reserved pear juice to measure 1 cup. Add to gelatin; stir until slightly thickened. Remove any unmelted ice; pour into blender container. Add cottage cheese, salt and ginger; cover. Blend until smooth. Stir in pears. Pour into 3 individual plastic containers or serving dishes. Chill until firm, about 2 hours.

Makes 3 cups or 3 entree servings

Nutrition Information Per Serving:

Calories	120	Fat	2 g
Cholesterol	5 mg	Carbohydrate	14 g
Sodium	480 mg	Protein	13 g

Diabetic Exchanges Per Serving:
1½ Lean Meat, 1 Fruit

Salad Veronique

Vegetable Cottage Cheese Salad

1 package (4-serving size)
   JELL-O Brand Lemon Flavor
   Sugar Free Gelatin
1 cup boiling water
¾ cup cold water
1 tablespoon vinegar
1 cup (8 ounces) 2% lowfat
   cottage cheese
¼ cup chopped celery
¼ cup chopped green pepper
¼ cup chopped red pepper
¼ cup chopped carrot
¼ teaspoon onion powder
⅛ teaspoon black pepper

- Completely dissolve gelatin in
  boiling water. Add cold water and
  vinegar. Measure 1 cup gelatin
  mixture; divide evenly among 3
  individual plastic containers or
  serving dishes. Chill until set but
  not firm. Add remaining
  ingredients to remaining gelatin.
  Chill until slightly thickened.
  Spoon over clear gelatin. Chill
  until firm, about 2 hours.

*Makes about 3¾ cups or
3 entree servings*

Nutrition Information Per Serving:

Calories	90	Fat	2 g
Cholesterol	5 mg	Carbohydrate	6 g
Sodium	410 mg	Protein	13 g

Diabetic Exchanges Per Serving:
1½ Lean Meat, 1 Vegetable

Neptune's Salad

2 packages (4-serving size
   each) or 1 package
   (8-serving size) JELL-O
   Brand Lemon Flavor Sugar
   Free Gelatin
2 cups boiling water
1 cup plain lowfat yogurt
2 tablespoons chili sauce
2 tablespoons finely chopped
   onion
2 tablespoons lemon juice
1 cup imitation crabmeat, flaked
½ cup chopped celery
¼ cup chopped red pepper

- Completely dissolve gelatin in
  boiling water. Stir in yogurt, chili
  sauce, onion and lemon juice.
  Chill until slightly thickened. Stir
  in remaining ingredients. Spoon
  into 4 individual plastic
  containers or serving dishes.
  Chill until firm, about 2 hours.

*Makes 5 cups or
4 entree servings*

Nutrition Information Per Serving:

Calories	110	Fat	2 g
Cholesterol	15 mg	Carbohydrate	12 g
Sodium	640 mg	Protein	12 g

Diabetic Exchanges Per Serving:
1 Lean Meat, ½ Nonfat Milk,
   1 Vegetable

Lemony Chicken Salad

1 can (13¾ ounces) low-sodium chicken broth
2 packages (4-serving size each) or 1 package (8-serving size) JELL-O Brand Lemon Flavor Sugar Free Gelatin
1 cup cold water
1 can (8 ounces) crushed pineapple in unsweetened juice, undrained
2 tablespoons lemon juice
½ teaspoon dried tarragon leaves, crushed
Dash of white pepper
1½ cups cubed cooked chicken breast
½ cup chopped celery
¼ cup chopped red pepper

- Bring chicken broth to a boil in small saucepan. Completely dissolve gelatin in boiling broth. Add water, pineapple, lemon juice, tarragon and white pepper. Chill until slightly thickened.

- Stir in chicken, celery and red pepper. Spoon into 4 individual plastic containers or serving dishes. Chill until firm, about 2 hours.

*Makes 5 cups or
4 entree servings*

Nutrition Information Per Serving:

Calories	160	Fat	3 g
Cholesterol	45 mg	Carbohydrate	11 g
Sodium	450 mg	Protein	22 g

Diabetic Exchanges Per Serving:
2 Lean Meat, 1 Vegetable

Tuna Dill Salad

1 package (4-serving size) JELL-O Brand Lemon Flavor Sugar Free Gelatin
¾ cup boiling water
½ cup cold water
1 tablespoon lemon juice
½ teaspoon dill weed
Dash of black pepper
¼ cup reduced-calorie sour cream
1 can (6½ ounces) tuna packed in water, drained and finely flaked
½ cup chopped celery
½ cup chopped red pepper
¼ cup sliced pitted ripe olives
2 tablespoons sliced green onions

- Completely dissolve gelatin in boiling water. Add cold water, lemon juice, dill and black pepper. Chill until slightly thickened. Blend in sour cream. Stir in remaining ingredients. Spoon into 3 individual plastic containers or serving dishes. Chill until firm, about 2 hours.

*Makes 3 cups or
3 entree servings*

Nutrition Information Per Serving:

Calories	130	Fat	4 g
Cholesterol	15 mg	Carbohydrate	4 g
Sodium	370 mg	Protein	17 g

Diabetic Exchanges Per Serving:
2 Lean Meat, 1 Vegetable

GOOD ENOUGH FOR GUESTS

Shh! Don't tell anyone that these are "diet" recipes. In fact, this chapter's recipes for "great beginnings" and "grand finales" make perfect party fare. As you can see by the photo on the opposite page, there is nothing diet-like about Chocolate Berry Trifle. It tastes as luscious as it looks. You'll also want to give both the Lovely Lemon cheesecake and Tiramisu a whirl. These two stupendous desserts are easily made in a blender.

In addition to desserts, you'll find some dynamic appetizers. Try our recipe for Seafood Dip. You and your guests will never guess that it "weighs in" at 70 calories per serving. Our Guacamole is the perfect solution for a make-ahead dip for guests—lemon juice and Sugar Free Lemon JELL-O Gelatin keep the avocado green. And, it has about two-thirds less fat than regular guacamole! We've also developed a simple lowfat recipe for Chili Tortilla Chips to serve on the side.

Next time you have company, give everyone's waistline a break and serve any one of these desserts and snacks. In fact, you might want to present a buffet of these tempting treats.

Chocolate Berry Trifle (page 60)

Chocolate Berry Trifle

This recipe is sure to get "oohs" and "aahs" whenever you serve it.

1½ cups cold 2% lowfat milk
1 package (4-serving size) JELL-O Chocolate Flavor Sugar Free Instant Pudding and Pie Filling
3¼ cups (8 ounces) COOL WHIP LITE Whipped Topping, thawed, divided
¼ cup low-sugar strawberry spread
1 package (10 ounces) ENTENMANN'S Fat Free Golden Loaf Cake, cut into 12 slices
1 cup raspberries
1 cup sliced strawberries

• Pour milk into large mixing bowl. Add pudding mix. Beat with wire whisk until well blended, 1 to 2 minutes. Gently stir in 1 cup of the whipped topping.

• Spread strawberry spread evenly over half of the cake slices. Top with the remaining cake slices; cut into ½-inch cubes. Place half of the cake cubes in large serving bowl; cover with half of the combined fruit. Top with 1 cup of the whipped topping and the pudding. Layer with the remaining cake cubes, fruit and whipped topping. Garnish if desired. Refrigerate until ready to serve.

Makes 12 servings

Nutrition Information Per Serving:

Calories	160	Fat	4 g
Cholesterol	5 mg	Carbohydrate	29 g
Sodium	240 mg	Protein	4 g

Diabetic Exchanges Per Serving:
1 Starch, 1 Fruit*, 1 Fat

*A fruit exchange is used to describe this recipe since most of its carbohydrate value comes from simple sugars. However, the recipe is not the nutritional equivalent of a fruit.

Frozen Cherry Terrine

Slice frozen loaf and freeze for a delicious snack.

1 can (8 ounces) pitted dark sweet cherries in light syrup, undrained
1 package (4-serving size) JELL-O Brand Cherry Flavor Sugar Free Gelatin
1 cup boiling water
1 container (8 ounces) plain lowfat yogurt
2 cups thawed COOL WHIP LITE Whipped Topping

• Line bottom and sides of 9×5-inch loaf pan with plastic wrap; set aside.

• Drain cherries, reserving syrup. If necessary, add enough cold water to reserved syrup to measure ½ cup. Cut cherries into quarters.

• Completely dissolve gelatin in boiling water. Add measured syrup. Stir in yogurt until well blended. Chill until mixture is thickened but not set, about 45 minutes to 1 hour, stirring occasionally. Gently stir in cherries and whipped topping.

Pour into prepared pan; cover. Freeze until firm, about 6 hours or overnight.

- Remove pan from freezer about 15 minutes before serving. Let stand at room temperature to soften slightly. Remove plastic wrap. Cut into slices.

Makes 12 servings

Note: Cover and store leftover terrine in freezer.

Nutrition Information Per Serving:

Calories	50	Fat	2 g
Cholesterol	0 mg	Carbohydrate	7 g
Sodium	45 mg	Protein	2 g

Diabetic Exchanges Per Serving:
½ Fruit, ½ Fat

Chilled Raspberry Souffle with Raspberry Sauce

1 package (4-serving size) JELL-O Brand Raspberry Flavor Sugar Free Gelatin
1 cup boiling water
1 package (10 ounces) BIRDS EYE Red Raspberries in a Lite Syrup, thawed, divided
½ cup cold water
1½ cups thawed COOL WHIP LITE Whipped Topping

- Completely dissolve gelatin in boiling water. Place raspberries in blender container; cover. Blend until pureed; strain. Stir ½ cup raspberry puree into gelatin. Add cold water. Chill until slightly thickened. Gently stir in whipped topping with wire whisk.

- Pour gelatin mixture evenly into six (6-ounce) custard cups or 3-cup souffle dish lined with a paper collar (see Note below). Chill until firm, about 3 hours.

- Unmold or remove collar. Serve souffle with the remaining raspberry puree.

Makes 3½ cups or 6 servings

Note: To make collar, cut a piece of wax paper or foil long enough to wrap around dish and overlap slightly; fold in half lengthwise. Wrap doubled paper around dish, extending about 1 inch above rim; secure with tape.

Nutrition Information Per Serving:

Calories	70	Fat	2 g
Cholesterol	0 mg	Carbohydrate	12 g
Sodium	50 mg	Protein	2 g

Diabetic Exchanges Per Serving:
1 Fruit, ½ Fat

Tiramisu

Tiramisu means "pick-me-up" in Italian and that is just what our version will do! Fresh sliced strawberries make a colorful addition.

1½ cups cold 2% lowfat milk, divided
1 container (8 ounces) pasteurized process cream cheese product
2 tablespoons MAXWELL HOUSE or YUBAN Instant Coffee or SANKA Brand 99.7% Caffeine Free Instant Coffee
1 tablespoon hot water
2 tablespoons brandy (optional)
1 package (4-serving size) JELL-O Vanilla Flavor Sugar Free Instant Pudding and Pie Filling
2 cups thawed COOL WHIP LITE Whipped Topping
1 package (3 ounces) ladyfingers, split
1 square (1 ounce) BAKER'S Semi-Sweet Chocolate, grated

- Pour ½ cup of the milk into blender container. Add cream cheese product; cover. Blend until smooth. Blend in the remaining 1 cup milk.

- Dissolve coffee in water; add to blender with brandy. Add pudding mix; cover. Blend until smooth, scraping down sides occasionally; pour into large bowl. Gently stir in whipped topping.

- Cut ladyfingers in half crosswise. Cover bottom of 8-inch springform pan with ladyfinger halves. Place remaining halves, cut-ends down, around sides of pan (see Photo 1). Spoon pudding mixture into pan. Chill until firm, about 3 hours. Remove side of pan. Sprinkle with grated chocolate (see Photo 2).

Makes 12 servings

Nutrition Information Per Serving:

Calories	140	Fat	6 g
Cholesterol	35 mg	Carbohydrate	15 g
Sodium	240 mg	Protein	4 g

Diabetic Exchanges Per Serving:
1½ Starch, 1 Fat

Photo 1

Photo 2

Tiramisu

Pinwheel Cake and Cream

A super-easy dessert that looks spectacular! Use your favorite combination of the following fruits: peaches, nectarines, plums, seedless grapes, strawberries, raspberries and blueberries. (The nutrition information for this recipe is based on the following 2 cups of fruit: 1/2 cup raspberries, 1/2 cup sliced strawberries, 1/2 cup seedless grapes and 1 medium peach, sliced.)

2 cups cold skim milk
1 package (4-serving size) JELL-O Vanilla Flavor Sugar Free Instant Pudding and Pie Filling
1 cup thawed COOL WHIP LITE Whipped Topping
1 small peach, peeled, chopped
1 teaspoon grated orange peel
1 package (10 ounces) ENTENMANN'S Fat Free Golden Loaf Cake, cut into slices
2 cups cut-up summer fruits

- Pour milk into medium mixing bowl. Add pudding mix. Beat with wire whisk until well blended, 1 to 2 minutes. Gently stir in whipped topping, peach and orange peel.

Arrange cake slices on serving plate. Spoon pudding mixture evenly over cake; top with fruits. Serve immediately or cover and refrigerate until ready to serve.

Makes 12 servings

Nutrition Information Per Serving:

Calories	120	Fat	1 g
Cholesterol	0 mg	Carbohydrate	25 g
Sodium	230 mg	Protein	3 g

Diabetic Exchanges Per Serving:
1 Fruit*, 1 Starch

*A fruit exchange is used to describe this recipe since most of its carbohydrate value comes from simple sugars. However, this recipe is not the nutritional equivalent of a fruit.

Pinwheel Cake and Cream

Lovely Lemon Cheesecake

For a no-mess way to make graham cracker crumbs for this cheesecake's crust, place graham cracker in plastic bag; roll with rolling pin to crush.

1 whole graham cracker, crushed, *or* **2 tablespoons graham cracker crumbs, divided**

1 package (4-serving size) JELL-O Brand Lemon Flavor Sugar Free Gelatin

⅔ cup boiling water

1 cup 1% lowfat cottage cheese

1 container (8 ounces) pasteurized process cream cheese product

2 cups thawed COOL WHIP LITE Whipped Topping

1 cup reduced-calorie cherry pie filling

- Spray 8- or 9-inch springform pan or 9-inch pie plate lightly with non-stick cooking spray. Sprinkle side with half of the graham cracker crumbs. (If desired, omit graham cracker crumb garnish; sprinkle bottom of pan with remaining graham cracker crumbs.)

- Completely dissolve gelatin in boiling water; pour into blender container. Add cottage cheese and cream cheese product; cover. Blend at medium speed, scraping down sides occasionally, about 2 minutes or until mixture is completely smooth. Pour into large bowl. Gently stir in whipped topping. Pour into prepared pan; smooth top. Sprinkle the remaining crumbs around outside edge. Chill until set, about 4 hours.

- When ready to serve, remove side of pan. Top cheesecake with pie filling.

Makes 8 servings

Nutrition Information Per Serving:

Calories	160	Fat	7 g
Cholesterol	15 mg	Carbohydrate	16 g
Sodium	330 mg	Protein	8 g

Diabetic Exchanges Per Serving:
1 Whole Milk, ½ Fruit*

---

*A fruit exchange is used to describe this recipe since most of its carbohydrate value comes from simple sugars. However, this recipe is not the nutritional equivalent of a fruit.

Orange Terrine with Strawberry Sauce

An elegant dessert for an elegant affair; garnish with fresh strawberries for extra pizzazz.

1 package (3 ounces) ladyfingers, split, divided
2 packages (4-serving size each) or 1 package (8-serving size) JELL-O Brand Orange Flavor Sugar Free Gelatin
1½ cups boiling water
1 cup cold orange juice Ice cubes
1 tablespoon orange liqueur (optional)
2 teaspoons grated orange peel
3¼ cups (8 ounces) COOL WHIP LITE Whipped Topping, thawed, divided
1 package (10 ounces) BIRDS EYE Strawberries in Syrup, thawed
1 cup fresh strawberries

• Line bottom and sides of 9×5-inch loaf pan with plastic wrap. Stand enough ladyfingers to fit evenly along 2 long sides of pan (cut sides should be facing in).

• Dissolve gelatin in boiling water. Combine orange juice and enough ice cubes to measure 1¾ cups. Add to gelatin; stir until slightly thickened. Remove any unmelted ice. Stir in liqueur and orange peel. Gently stir in 2½ cups of the whipped topping.

• Spoon gelatin mixture into prepared pan. If necessary, trim ladyfingers to make even with top of gelatin mixture. Arrange remaining ladyfingers evenly on top of gelatin mixture. Chill until firm, at least 3 hours.

• When ready to serve, place thawed frozen strawberries in blender container; cover. Blend until pureed; strain. Unmold terrine onto serving plate; remove plastic wrap. Decorate with the remaining ¾ cup whipped topping and fresh strawberries. Cut into slices. Serve on strawberry puree.

Makes 12 servings

Nutrition Information Per Serving:

Calories	100	Fat	3 g
Cholesterol	25 mg	Carbohydrate	15 g
Sodium	60 mg	Protein	2 g

Diabetic Exchanges Per Serving:
1 Fruit, 1 Fat

Orange Terrine with Strawberry Sauce

Belgian Waffle Dessert

An excellent choice for a brunch dessert, the berries provide an added bonus of 2 grams of fiber per serving.

2¼ cups cold 2% lowfat milk
1 package (4-serving size) JELL-O Vanilla Flavor Sugar Free Instant Pudding and Pie Filling
2 tablespoons lemon juice
1 teaspoon grated lemon peel
1 cup thawed COOL WHIP LITE Whipped Topping
10 small frozen Belgian or regular waffles, toasted
2 cups strawberries, sliced
1 cup raspberries
1 cup blueberries or blackberries

- Pour milk into large mixing bowl. Add pudding mix, lemon juice and peel. Beat with wire whisk until well blended, 1 to 2 minutes. Gently stir in whipped topping.

- For each dessert, spoon about 3 tablespoons pudding mixture onto each dessert plate; top with waffle, an additional 2 tablespoons pudding mixture and a scant ½ cup combined fruits. Garnish if desired. Repeat for remaining desserts as needed. Store any leftover pudding mixture and fruit in refrigerator.

Makes 10 servings

Nutrition Information Per Serving:

Calories	170	Fat	5 g
Cholesterol	5 mg	Carbohydrate	27 g
Sodium	310 mg	Protein	4 g

Diabetic Exchanges Per Serving:
1 Starch, 1 Fruit, 1 Fat

Cheese "Danish"

You might be surprised to learn that a flour tortilla forms the shell for these inspired pastry-like desserts. For a festive touch, we've decorated the serving plate with raspberries and mint.

1 tablespoon sugar
1 teaspoon ground cinnamon
5 (6- to 7-inch) flour tortillas Non-stick cooking spray
1 cup cold skim milk
1 package (4-serving size) JELL-O Vanilla Flavor Sugar Free Instant Pudding and Pie Filling
1 container (8 ounces) pasteurized process cream cheese product
2 cups thawed COOL WHIP LITE Whipped Topping
1 square (1 ounce) BAKER'S Semi-Sweet Chocolate

- Heat oven to 350°F.

- Combine sugar and cinnamon. Spray tortillas with non-stick cooking spray. Sprinkle each tortilla with a scant ½ teaspoon cinnamon-sugar mixture. Turn tortillas over; repeat. Cut each tortilla into 4 wedges. Stand rounded edge of each tortilla wedge in bottom of muffin cup, curling sides in to fit cup (see Photo 1, page 72). Bake 10 minutes or until crisp and lightly browned. Cool in pan.

(continued)

Top to bottom: Cheese "Danish"; Belgian Waffle Dessert

- Pour milk into large mixing bowl. Add pudding mix. Beat at low speed with electric mixer until well blended, 1 to 2 minutes. Beat in cream cheese product at medium speed until smooth. Gently stir in whipped topping. Refrigerate until chilled, at least 1 hour.

Photo 1

- When ready to serve, fill each tortilla shell with a scant 3 tablespoons pudding mixture, using pastry bag or spoon (see Photo 2). Place chocolate in small freezer-weight zippered plastic bag. Microwave on HIGH 1 minute or until chocolate is melted. Fold over top of bag tightly; snip off one tiny corner (about 1/8 inch) from bottom of bag. Holding bag tightly at top, drizzle chocolate over desserts (see Photo 3). Refrigerate until chocolate sets, about 5 minutes.

Photo 2

Makes 20 servings

Note: Cover and freeze any leftover desserts. Thaw in refrigerator as needed.

Photo 3

Nutrition Information Per Serving (1 "Danish"):			
Calories	90	Fat	4 g
Cholesterol	5 mg	Carbohydrate	10 g
Sodium	180 mg	Protein	3 g

Diabetic Exchanges Per Serving:
1/2 Starch, 1 Fat

Herbed Cheese Dip

- 1 package (4-serving size) JELL-O Brand Lemon Flavor Sugar Free Gelatin
- ¼ teaspoon salt
- 1 cup boiling water
- 1 container (16 ounces) 2% lowfat cottage cheese
- 4 ounces neufchatel cheese
- ½ cup packed fresh parsley sprigs
- 2 garlic cloves
- 2 tablespoons vinegar
- 2 teaspoons dill weed
- 1 teaspoon Worcestershire sauce
- ½ teaspoon pepper

• Completely dissolve gelatin and salt in boiling water; pour into blender container. Add remaining ingredients; cover. Blend at low speed, scraping down sides occasionally, 2 minutes or until mixture is smooth. Pour into serving bowl. Chill until set, about 4 hours.

Makes 3½ cups or 12 servings

Nutrition Information Per Serving:
Calories 60 Fat 3 g
Cholesterol 10 mg Carbohydrate 2 g
Sodium 260 mg Protein 7 g

Diabetic Exchanges Per Serving:
1 Lean Meat

Seafood Dip

This molded dip is a sought-after solution for a rich-tasting, yet low-fat appetizer. Garnish with dill and red pepper strips, if desired.

- 1 package (4-serving size) JELL-O Brand Lemon Flavor Sugar Free Gelatin
- ¾ cup boiling water
- 1 container (8 ounces) plain lowfat yogurt
- 1 container (8 ounces) reduced-calorie sour cream
- ½ cup cocktail sauce
- 2 tablespoons lemon juice
- ½ pound imitation crabmeat, chopped
- 1 cup chopped celery
- ¼ cup finely chopped onion
- 1½ teaspoons dill weed

• Completely dissolve gelatin in boiling water. Stir in yogurt, sour cream, cocktail sauce and lemon juice until well blended. Chill until thickened, 20 to 25 minutes.

• Stir in imitation crabmeat, celery, onion and dill weed until well blended. Pour into 5-cup mold which has been lightly sprayed with non-stick cooking spray. Chill until set, about 3 hours. Unmold. Serve with vegetable sticks or lowfat crackers.

Makes 4⅔ cups or 14 servings

Nutrition Information Per Serving:
Calories 70 Fat 2 g
Cholesterol 10 mg Carbohydrate 6 g
Sodium 280 mg Protein 4 g

Diabetic Exchanges Per Serving:
½ Whole Milk

Guacamole

Guacamole and chips on a diet? You bet, when they are made with these tasty recipes.

1 package (4-serving size) JELL-O Brand Lemon Flavor Sugar Free Gelatin
1 cup boiling water
1 container (16 ounces) 1% lowfat cottage cheese
1 cup chopped ripe avocado
¾ cup chopped green onions, divided
¼ cup drained pickled jalapeño pepper slices
¼ cup lemon juice
2 garlic cloves
1 to 2 teaspoons chili powder
¼ cup finely chopped tomato
4 pitted ripe olives, sliced

- Completely dissolve gelatin in boiling water; pour into blender container. Add cottage cheese, avocado, ½ cup of the green onions, the jalapeño peppers, lemon juice, garlic and chili powder; cover. Blend on low speed, scraping down sides occasionally, about 2 minutes or until mixture is smooth. Pour into shallow 5-cup serving dish; smooth top. Chill until set, about 4 hours.

- When ready to serve, top guacamole with the remaining ¼ cup chopped green onion, the tomato and olives. Serve as a dip with Chili Tortilla Chips (recipe follows) or fresh vegetables.

Makes about 3⅓ cups or 10 servings

Nutrition Information Per Serving:

Calories	70	Fat	3 g
Cholesterol	0 mg	Carbohydrate	4 g
Sodium	280 mg	Protein	7 g

Diabetic Exchanges Per Serving:
½ Medium Fat Meat, 1 Vegetable

Chili Tortilla Chips

These chips are lower in calories than regular tortilla chips because they are baked, not fried.

6 (7-inch) flour tortillas
Non-stick cooking spray
Chili powder

- Heat oven to 350°F.

- Lightly spray tortillas with non-stick cooking spray; sprinkle with chili powder. Turn tortillas over; repeat. Cut each tortilla into 8 wedges; place on cookie sheet. Bake 8 to 10 minutes until crisp and lightly browned.

Makes 48 chips or 12 servings

Nutrition Information Per Serving (4 chips):

Calories	60	Fat	1 g
Cholesterol	0 mg	Carbohydrate	10 g
Sodium	90 mg	Protein	2 g

Diabetic Exchanges Per Serving:
1 Starch

Guacamole with Chili Tortilla Chips

ALL-AMERICAN FAMILY CLASSICS

We think it's a toss-up—JELL-O might just be more American than apple pie! Way back in 1845, good old American ingenuity inspired Peter Cooper to create a gelatin dessert which was later named JELL-O. Since then, JELL-O Brand Gelatin has continued to grow in popularity. Today it can be found in over half the homes in the United States and has truly become an American classic.

The 1980's brought the development of Sugar Free JELL-O Gelatin and Pudding. Using these two products, our test kitchen experts have created the "homey" desserts found in this chapter. Some of the recipes, like Ribbon Mold, are classic JELL-O recipes that have been adapted to be lower in calories and fat. Other recipes, such as Spiced Cranberry-Orange Mold and Apple Walnut Bread Pudding, are American classics that we have slimmed down and sparked up with some innovative new twists.

If you're looking for some surefire recipes to please both you and your family, turn to this chapter for recipes you'll want to include every day.

Spiced Cranberry-Orange Mold
(page 78)

Spiced Cranberry-Orange Mold

This mold is too good to serve only during the holidays.

2 packages (4-serving size each) or 1 package (8-serving size) JELL-O Brand Raspberry Flavor Sugar Free Gelatin
¼ teaspoon salt
1½ cups boiling water
1 can (16 ounces) whole berry cranberry sauce
½ cup cold water
1 tablespoon lemon juice
¼ teaspoon ground cinnamon
⅛ teaspoon ground cloves
1 orange, peeled, sectioned and finely chopped

- Completely dissolve gelatin and salt in boiling water. Add cranberry sauce, cold water, lemon juice, cinnamon and cloves. Chill until slightly thickened.

- Stir in orange. Spoon into 5-cup mold which has been lightly sprayed with non-stick cooking spray. Chill until firm, about 4 hours. Unmold. Garnish if desired.

Makes about 5 cups or 10 servings

Nutrition Information Per Serving:
Calories 80 Fat 0 g
Cholesterol 0 mg Carbohydrate 19 g
Sodium 115 mg Protein 1 g

Diabetic Exchanges Per Serving:
1½ Fruit

Apple Walnut Bread Pudding

4 slices firm-textured white bread
2 teaspoons margarine, melted
2 medium apples, chopped
¼ cup chopped walnuts
2 cups cold 2% lowfat milk
½ cup thawed frozen egg substitute
1 teaspoon vanilla
1 package (4-serving size) JELL-O Vanilla Flavor Sugar Free Pudding and Pie Filling
1 teaspoon ground cinnamon, divided

- Heat oven to 350°F.

- Lightly brush bread slices with margarine; cut into ½-inch cubes. Place on cookie sheet. Bake 10 minutes or until lightly toasted. Place in shallow 1½-quart baking dish. Add apples and walnuts; toss lightly.

- Pour milk, egg substitute and vanilla into large mixing bowl. Beat with wire whisk until well blended. Add pudding mix and ½ teaspoon of the cinnamon; whisk until well blended. Pour over bread mixture; sprinkle with the remaining ½ teaspoon cinnamon. Bake 30 minutes. Remove from oven; let stand 10 minutes before serving.

Makes 8 servings

Nutrition Information Per Serving:
Calories 130 Fat 5 g
Cholesterol 5 mg Carbohydrate 17 g
Sodium 190 mg Protein 5 g

Diabetic Exchanges Per Serving:
1 Starch, 1 Fat

Apple Walnut Bread Puddin

Ribbon Mold

Try this mold with other flavor combinations. For more flavor and only 5 extra calories per serving, you can use vanilla lowfat yogurt in place of the plain lowfat yogurt.

2 packages (4-serving size each) or 1 package (8-serving size) JELL-O Brand Strawberry Flavor Sugar Free Gelatin
5 cups boiling water, divided
⅔ cup plain lowfat yogurt, divided
2 packages (4-serving size each) or 1 package (8-serving size) JELL-O Brand Lime Flavor Sugar Free Gelatin

Completely dissolve strawberry flavor gelatin in 2½ cups of the boiling water. Pour 1½ cups of the dissolved gelatin into 6-cup ring mold which has been lightly sprayed with non-stick cooking spray. Chill until set but not firm, about 30 minutes. Meanwhile, chill remaining gelatin in bowl until slightly thickened; gradually blend in ⅓ cup of the yogurt. Spoon over gelatin in mold. Chill until set but not firm, about 15 minutes.

Repeat process with lime flavor gelatin, the remaining 2½ cups boiling water and the remaining ⅓ cup yogurt. Chill 1½ cups dissolved lime flavor gelatin until thoroughly cooled before pouring into mold. (Warm gelatin mixture could soften the layer beneath it and cause mixtures to run

together.) Chill until set, about 2 hours. Unmold.
Makes 6 cups or 12 servings

Nutrition Information Per Serving:
Calories	20	Fat	0 g
Cholesterol	0 mg	Carbohydrate	1 g
Sodium	95 mg	Protein	3 g

Diabetic Exchanges Per Serving:
Free, Limited

Watergate Salad

This is a slimmed-down version of a favorite classic recipe.

1 package (4-serving size) JELL-O Pistachio Flavor Sugar Free Instant Pudding and Pie Filling
1 can (20 ounces) crushed pineapple in unsweetened juice, undrained
½ cup miniature marshmallows
¼ cup chopped walnuts
1½ cups thawed COOL WHIP LITE Whipped Topping

• Combine pudding mix, pineapple, marshmallows and nuts in large bowl; mix well. Gently stir in whipped topping; refrigerate until ready to serve.
Makes 3½ cups or 7 servings

Nutrition Information Per Serving:
Calories	130	Fat	5 g
Cholesterol	0 mg	Carbohydrate	23 g
Sodium	200 mg	Protein	2 g

Diabetic Exchanges Per Serving:
1½ Fruit, 1 Fat

Ribbon Mold

Pear Fans with Creamy Custard Sauce

8 canned pear halves in juice, drained
Creamy Custard Sauce (see recipe this page)
8 raspberries
8 mint leaves

- Cut pear halves into thin slices with sharp knife, cutting up to but not through stem ends. Holding stem end in place, gently fan out slices from stem. Place on dessert plates. Spoon about 1/3 cup Creamy Custard Sauce around pears. Place a raspberry and mint leaf at stem end of each pear.

Makes 8 servings

Nutrition Information Per Serving:

Calories	100	Fat	2 g
Cholesterol	10 mg	Carbohydrate	17 g
Sodium	210 mg	Protein	3 g

Diabetic Exchanges Per Serving:
1/2 2% Lowfat Milk, 1 Fruit

Creamy Custard Sauce

This creamy sauce can be used for multitude of purposes. Try it with fresh fruit.

3 cups cold 2% lowfat milk
1 package (4-serving size) JELL-O Vanilla Flavor Suga Free Instant Pudding and Pie Filling
1/4 teaspoon ground cinnamon (optional)

- Pour milk into large mixing bowl Add pudding mix and cinnamon Beat with wire whisk until well blended, 1 to 2 minutes; cover. Refrigerate until ready to serve.

Makes 3 cups or 8 serving

Note: Refrigerate any leftover sauce. Thin with small amount of additional milk before serving, if desired.

Nutrition Information Per Serving:

Calories	60	Fat	2 g
Cholesterol	10 mg	Carbohydrate	7 g
Sodium	210 mg	Protein	3 g

Diabetic Exchanges Per Serving:
1/2 2% Lowfat Milk

Top to bottom: Creamy Custard Sauc
Pear Fans with Creamy Custard Sau

Peach Melba Dessert

**2 packages (4-serving size
   each) or 1 package
   (8-serving size) JELL-O
   Brand Raspberry Flavor
   Sugar Free Gelatin, divided**
1½ cups boiling water, divided
**1 container (8 ounces) vanilla
   lowfat yogurt**
½ cup raspberries
**1 can (8 ounces) sliced peaches
   packed in juice, undrained
   Cold water**

• Completely dissolve 1 package
  of the gelatin in ¾ cup of the
  boiling water; chill until slightly
  thickened. Stir in yogurt and
  raspberries. Pour into medium
  serving bowl; chill until set but
  not firm.

Completely dissolve the
remaining package of gelatin in
the remaining ¾ cup boiling
water. Drain peaches, reserving
juice. Add enough cold water to
reserved juice to measure 1 cup.
Add to dissolved gelatin; chill
until slightly thickened.

Reserve a few peaches for
garnish, if desired. Chop
remaining peaches; stir into
slightly thickened gelatin. Spoon
over creamy layer in bowl. Chill
until firm, about 3 hours. Top with
reserved peach slices. Garnish if
desired.

Makes 4 cups or 8 servings

Nutrition Information Per Serving:

Calories	50	Fat	0 g
Cholesterol	0 mg	Carbohydrate	9 g
Sodium	80 mg	Protein	3 g

Diabetic Exchanges Per Serving:
1 Fruit

Creamy Brown Rice Pudding

*This creamy pudding is satisfying
when served either warm or cold.
Make sure to use Cook'n Serve
pudding & pie filling mix and **not**
instant pudding mix.*

**3 cups cold 2% lowfat milk,
   divided**
**¾ cup MINUTE Instant Brown
   Rice**
**1 package (4-serving size)
   JELL-O Sugar Free Vanilla
   Pudding and Pie Filling**
¼ cup raisins
⅛ teaspoon ground cinnamon

• Bring 1 cup of the milk to a boil in
  medium saucepan. Stir in rice.
  Return to a full boil. Cover;
  reduce heat. Simmer 5 minutes.
  Stir in the remaining 2 cups milk,
  the pudding mix, raisins and
  cinnamon. Bring to a boil over
  medium heat, stirring constantly.
  Remove from heat; cover. Let
  stand 5 minutes. Stir; cool
  slightly. Serve warm, sprinkled
  with additional cinnamon, if
  desired. (Or, place plastic wrap
  directly on surface of hot
  pudding and refrigerate at least
  30 minutes.)

Makes 3⅓ cups or 6 servings

Nutrition Information Per Serving:

Calories	140	Fat	3 g
Cholesterol	10 mg	Carbohydrate	23 g
Sodium	160 mg	Protein	5 g

Diabetic Exchanges Per Serving:
½ 2% Lowfat Milk, 1 Starch

Peach Melba Dessert

SUPER SHAKES

No matter what time of day it is, a cool creamy shake could be just the slimming treat you crave when you are counting calories. The shakes in this chapter are especially great because you make a big batch all at once in the blender. Pour out a single serving, and store the remaining servings in the blender container in the refrigerator. When you want a shake, just give the mixture a quick spin in the blender and it's ready. Each shake will keep for up to a week if you make sure to use very fresh milk that has an expiration date that is later than a week after you make the recipe.

While we've given directions for scrumptious shakes, including Strawberry Banana Yogurt Shake, Easy Chocolate Pudding Milk Shake and Cherry Banana Shake, don't hesitate to experiment and come up with your own flavor combinations. An added bonus is that all of these recipes are made with skim or lowfat milk which are good sources of calcium.

Top right to bottom left: Orange M
Shake (page 88); Strawberry Bana
Yogurt Shake (page 88); Ea
Chocolate Pudding Milk Sha
(page 8

Easy Chocolate Pudding Milk Shake

For double chocolate impact, use chocolate ice milk instead of vanilla ice milk.

3 cups cold skim milk
1 package (4-serving size) JELL-O Chocolate Flavor Sugar Free Instant Pudding and Pie Filling
1½ cups vanilla ice milk

• Pour milk into blender container. Add remaining ingredients; cover. Blend at high speed 15 seconds or until smooth. (Mixture thickens as it stands. Thin with additional milk, if desired.)
   Makes about 5 cups or 5 servings

Nutrition Information Per Serving:

Calories	150	Fat	2 g
Cholesterol	10 mg	Carbohydrate	23 g
Sodium	370 mg	Protein	7 g

Diabetic Exchanges Per Serving:
½ 2% Lowfat Milk, 1 Starch

Strawberry Banana Yogurt Shake

Quick, refreshing, wholesome snack.

2 cups cold skim milk
1 package (4-serving size) JELL-O Brand Strawberry Flavor Sugar Free Gelatin
1 container (8 ounces) plain lowfat yogurt
1 cup crushed ice
1 large banana, cut into chunks

• Pour milk into blender container. Add remaining ingredients; cover. Blend at high speed 30 seconds or until smooth.
   Makes 5 cups or 5 servings

Nutrition Information Per Serving:

Calories	100	Fat	1 g
Cholesterol	5 mg	Carbohydrate	14 g
Sodium	130 mg	Protein	7 g

Diabetic Exchanges Per Serving:
½ Nonfat Milk, ½ Fruit

Orange Milk Shake

2 cups cold skim milk
1 package (4-serving size) JELL-O Brand Orange Flavor Sugar Free Gelatin
1 cup vanilla ice milk

• Pour milk into blender container. Add remaining ingredients; cover. Blend at high speed 30 seconds or until smooth.
   Makes 4 cups or 4 servings

Nutrition Information Per Serving:

Calories	100	Fat	2 g
Cholesterol	10 mg	Carbohydrate	14 g
Sodium	150 mg	Protein	7 g

Diabetic Exchanges Per Serving:
½ 2% Lowfat Milk, ½ Starch

Chocolate Peanut Butter Shake

3½ cups cold skim milk
1 package (4-serving size)
    JELL-O Chocolate Flavor
    Sugar Free Instant Pudding
    and Pie Filling
1 cup chocolate ice milk
2 tablespoons creamy peanut
    butter

- Pour milk into blender container. Add remaining ingredients; cover. Blend at high speed 15 seconds or until smooth. (Mixture thickens as it stands. Thin with additional milk, if desired.)
    Makes 5 cups or 5 servings

Nutrition Information Per Serving:

Calories	180	Fat	5 g
Cholesterol	10 mg	Carbohydrate	23 g
Sodium	400 mg	Protein	9 g

Diabetic Exchanges Per Serving:
½ Whole Milk, 1 Starch

Peachy Pudding Shake

3 cups cold skim milk
1 package (4-serving size)
    JELL-O Vanilla Flavor Sugar
    Free Instant Pudding and
    Pie Filling
2 cups frozen peach slices

- Pour milk into blender container. Add remaining ingredients; cover. Blend at high speed 30 seconds or until smooth. (Mixture thickens as it stands. Thin with additional milk, if desired.)
    Makes 5 cups or 5 servings

Nutrition Information Per Serving:

Calories	100	Fat	0 g
Cholesterol	5 mg	Carbohydrate	19 g
Sodium	340 mg	Protein	6 g

Diabetic Exchanges Per Serving:
½ Nonfat Milk, 1 Fruit

Mint Chocolate Chip Milk Shake

3 cups cold skim milk
1 package (4-serving size)
   JELL-O Pistachio Flavor
   Sugar Free Instant Pudding
   and Pie Filling
1½ cups vanilla ice milk
   ¼ teaspoon peppermint extract
   ½ square (½ ounce) BAKER'S
   Semi-Sweet Chocolate,
   grated (page 62)

• Pour milk into blender container. Add pudding mix, ice milk and extract; cover. Blend at high speed 15 seconds or until smooth. (Mixture thickens as it stands. Thin with additional milk, if desired.) Sprinkle individual servings with grated chocolate.

Makes 5 cups or 5 servings

Nutrition Information Per Serving:

Calories	150	Fat	3 g
Cholesterol	10 mg	Carbohydrate	24 g
Sodium	380 mg	Protein	7 g

Diabetic Exchanges Per Serving:
½ 2% Lowfat Milk, 1 Starch

Easy Peanut Butter Milk Shake

3 cups cold skim milk
1 package (4-serving size)
   JELL-O Butterscotch Flavor
   Sugar Free Instant Pudding
   and Pie Filling
1½ cups vanilla ice milk
   2 tablespoons creamy peanut
   butter

• Pour milk into blender container. Add remaining ingredients; cover. Blend at high speed 15 seconds or until smooth. (Mixture thickens as it stands. Thin with additional milk, if desired.)

Makes 5 cups or 5 servings

Nutrition Information Per Serving:

Calories	170	Fat	5 g
Cholesterol	10 mg	Carbohydrate	23 g
Sodium	410 mg	Protein	9 g

Diabetic Exchanges Per Serving:
½ Whole Milk, 1 Starch

Chocolate Fudge Shake

Surprisingly low in calories with big chocolate flavor.

**2 cups cold 2% lowfat milk
1 package (4-serving size)
    JELL-O Chocolate Fudge
    Flavor Sugar Free Instant
    Pudding and Pie Filling
2 cups crushed ice**

- Pour milk into blender container. Add remaining ingredients; cover. Blend at high speed 15 seconds or until smooth. (Mixture thickens as it stands. Thin with additional milk, if desired.)
    Makes 4 cups or 4 servings

Nutrition Information Per Serving:
Calories   100 Fat   3 g
Cholesterol 10 mg Carbohydrate 14 g
Sodium   340 mg Protein   5 g

Diabetic Exchanges Per Serving:
½ 2% Lowfat Milk, ½ Starch

Raspberry Cream Shake

**1 cup cold skim milk
1 package (4-serving size)
    JELL-O Brand Raspberry
    Flavor Sugar Free Gelatin
1 cup vanilla ice milk
1 cup crushed ice
½ cup raspberries**

- Pour milk into blender container. Add remaining ingredients; cover. Blend at high speed 30 seconds or until smooth.
    Makes 3½ cups or 3 servings

Nutrition Information Per Serving:
Calories   120 Fat   2 g
Cholesterol 10 mg Carbohydrate 18 g
Sodium   160 mg Protein   7 g

Diabetic Exchanges Per Serving:
½ Nonfat Milk, 1 Starch

Cherry Banana Shake

**1 cup cold skim milk
1 package (4-serving size)
    JELL-O Brand Cherry Flavor
    Sugar Free Gelatin
1 cup crushed ice
1 large banana, cut into chunks**

- Pour milk into blender container. Add remaining ingredients; cover. Blend at high speed 30 seconds or until smooth.
    Makes 3 cups or 3 servings

Nutrition Information Per Serving:
Calories   80 Fat   0 g
Cholesterol 0 mg Carbohydrate 14 g
Sodium   130 mg Protein   5 g

Diabetic Exchanges Per Serving:
½ Nonfat Milk, ½ Fruit

CALORIE INDEX

Calories Per Serving	Recipe Title and Page
8	Sparkling Lemon Ice, 26
10	JELL-O JIGGLERS, 24
14	Melon Bubbles, 16
14	JELL-O JIGGLERS Yogurt Snacks, 24
16	Three Pepper Salad, 45
18	Muffin Pan Snacks, 19
20	Ribbon Mold, 81
25	Fruit Sparkles, 23
25	Gazpacho Salad, 42
30	Citrus Sensation, 19
30	Orange Onion Salad, 47
30	Quick Berry Parfaits, 20
35	Fresh Fruit Parfaits, 20
40	Carrot Raisin Salad, 45
40	Sunset Yogurt Salad, 47
50	Creamy Yogurt Cups, 24
50	Frozen Cherry Terrine, 60
50	Peach Melba Dessert, 85
50	White Sangria Splash, 48
60	Applesauce Snack Cups, 29
60	Cherry Waldorf Salad, 48
60	Chili Tortilla Chips, 75
60	Chocolate Banana Pops, 37
60	Creamy Custard Sauce, 82
60	Herbed Cheese Dip, 73
70	Cherry Almond Supreme, 26
70	Chilled Raspberry Souffle with Raspberry Sauce, 61
70	Guacamole, 75
70	Seafood Dip, 73
80	Cherry Banana Shake, 91
80	Fruited Gelatin and Cottage Cheese, 23
80	Spiced Cranberry-Orange Mold, 78
90	Cheese "Danish," 70
90	Chocolate Mousse, 38
90	Mocha-Spice Dessert, 38
90	Vegetable Cottage Cheese Salad, 56
100	Chef's Salad, 52
100	Chocolate Fudge Shake, 91
100	Chocolate Pudding Sandwiches, 35
100	Orange Milk Shake, 88
100	Orange Terrine with Strawberry Sauce, 69
100	Peachy Pudding Shake, 89
100	Pear Fans with Creamy Custard Sauce, 82
100	Salad Veronique, 55
100	Sparkling Berry Salad, 42
100	Strawberry Banana Yogurt Shake, 88
100	Tuna Nicoise, 53
110	Ambrosia Parfaits, 29
110	Chocolate Peanut Butter Parfaits, 32
110	Neptune's Salad, 56
120	Cherries Jubilee, 16
120	Chocolate Bread Pudding, 34
120	Chocolate Cookie Crumble, 35
120	Chocolate Raspberry Cheesecake, 34
120	Gingered Pear Salad, 55
120	Pinwheel Cake and Cream, 65
120	Raspberry Cream Shake, 91
120	Vanilla Pudding Grahamwiches, 37
130	Apple Walnut Bread Pudding, 78
130	Tuna Dill Salad, 57
130	Watergate Salad, 81
140	Creamy Brown Rice Pudding, 85
140	Taco Salad, 52
140	Tiramisu, 62
150	Easy Chocolate Pudding Milk Shake, 88
150	Mint Chocolate Chip Milk Shake, 90
160	Dijon Chicken Salad, 53
160	Chocolate Berry Trifle, 60
160	Lemony Chicken Salad, 57
160	Lovely Lemon Cheesecake, 66
170	Belgian Waffle Dessert, 70
170	Easy Peanut Butter Milk Shake, 90
180	Chocolate Peanut Butter Shake, 89
190	Black Forest Parfaits, 32

RECIPE INDEX

NOTES